Now What Do I Say?

Never Be At a Loss For Words Again:
Real Estate Objection Handlers
for Virtually Every Situation

by
Scott Friedman, Christy Crouch, Donna Fleetwood

ISBN: 1-4196-9566-5

ISBN-13: 9781419695667

Visit www.booksurge.com to order additional copies.

Now What Do I Say?

Never Be At a Loss For Words Again:
Real Estate Objection Handlers
for Virtually Every Situation

Table of Contents

Introduction
The Secrets to Objection Handling
Objections and Handlers

Introduction

What's one of the biggest challenges you face as a real estate agent? It's knowing what to say and how to say it, isn't it?

With over forty-five years combined experience in real estate sales and training, we've come to realize one thing:

You're going to get objections.

All sellers want to find a house to buy before they list, save on commission, price their properties higher, list for 30 days, have you do tons of advertising, open houses, etc. All buyers say they're "good" without talking to a lender, want to look before being qualified, want to wait until the market is right, want you to cut your commission to make the deal work; and the list goes on.

Since you're going to get objections, wouldn't it be great if you could powerfully and confidently handle them?

In this book we show you the secrets to objection handling, and give you some of the most effective objection handlers for virtually every situation you'll come across in real estate sales.

Good objection handling skills naturally make appointments fun, exciting and remind you of why you got into sales.

The ideas and content in this book will undoubtedly help to increase your business and melt away the resistance that you experience.

Using this book will give you the confidence and power to handle any question or objection that you face. Keep this book with you, so you can refer back to it time and again, and it will take your business to new heights!

The Secrets to Objection Handling

Although the handlers in this book will immediately impact your business, simply having the scripts, or the words to say, isn't always enough. There are a number of secrets to handling objections.

You need to realize where objections come from. They only come from people who are considering doing business with you. If they didn't want to do business with you, they wouldn't object. It wouldn't be worth their time. So getting an objection is actually a good thing.

Why do people object, stonewall and defer decisions that will ultimately be the best thing for them? The answer is always: **fear**. They are afraid, and want to feel they have an advocate for their decisions, their dreams, and most importantly, the dollar in their pocket. When you call a For Sale By Owner, they fear that you are going to take that dollar out of their pocket. We know that, time after time, we can actually make a seller more money and get them moved faster than they can on their own.

And they'll never believe that unless you believe in what you are saying. If you are not telling them the truth, they will get uncomfortable and never sign on the dotted line. As you study the objection handlers in this book, be very aware of how your personal beliefs might sabotage your success.

Remember when handling objections, people don't care how much you know until they know how much you care. Put their needs, wants and desires above your own. When you come from a place of true care and concern for your client, they automatically feel it. That alone can make the difference between getting the sale and not getting the sale.

When handling objections you will typically want to align with, acknowledge and accept your client's objection and let them know you are on their side. Defending obviously puts you on the other side. You want to be with them -- not against them. **Never argue with a prospect or client.**

People like people who are like themselves. Immediately look people in the eye if you are in person, watch their body language and put your focus on them instead of yourself. The more you align and build rapport with your clients, the better chance you have of them choosing you over your competition.

In most cases, you need to approve what the speaker says, and sometimes repeat it before actually handling the objection. This makes sure they feel heard. Most of our handlers in this book feature approval and/or repetition.

Clients aren't coming up with new real estate objections. If you've been in business for some time, you already know the objections that you typically get. If you're just starting out, this book will help you tremendously because we have taken the most common objections you will get in your business. Regardless of how long you've been in the business, don't be surprised, or caught off guard anymore when you get an objection. Simply realize that objections are a natural part of your job, and practice handling them.

Whether you practice the handlers from this book or create your own, role play in front of a mirror or with partners. It is imperative that you practice them to the point of memorization.

Practicing will give you lots of confidence, alleviate your fears and allow you to relax. Your confidence and enthusiasm will show through and, more often than not, actually handle many objections before they are even voiced.

Knowing the difference between an objection and a condition is critical. Simply put, an objection is something that, if handled properly, can lead to a sale or signed contract. A condition is a roadblock; you cannot get around it. Asking you to cut your commission is an objection. Not moving until their child finishes high school is a condition.

Keep these secrets in mind and refer to this book often, so that you become a master at handling objections.

DISCLAIMER

Some of the handlers in this book state hypothetical statistics, e.g.: "…I sold 20 homes in the last six months…," and "…the average home in this market takes 164 days to sell…," etc. The use of market data when handling objections can be very powerful. However, as a professional, it is extremely important for you to research and know your industry, your market, your office and your personal statistics. Usually, you can find this information through your local real estate board. We **do not** advocate or condone misleading anyone with false information and/or statistics.

Now What Do I Say?

CALLING EXPIRED LISTINGS

1.   I'm going to take it off the market for now.

I can appreciate that you want to take it off the market. So what would happen if you left it on and got it sold this time? Because the market is obviously not great, and the more time you take, the more money you could lose. And if you'd be willing to meet with me, I'd be willing to show you how I sold 20 homes in the last six months for top dollar. Do you want top dollar?

That makes sense. And I'm curious, what will <u>not</u> being on the market accomplish for you?

That makes sense. I bet you're tired of having people traipse through your home and it not selling, aren't you? Imagine for a moment that you put the home on the market with an active and aggressive agent, like me, who could actually get the home sold, and help you move forward? Having sold 20 homes so far this year, I am definitely confident that I could get your home sold and certainly would take excellent care of you. What would be a good time for me to come by and show you how I can help you?

I can understand that you want to keep it off the market. And since the market is flattening out even more, shouldn't you consider selling now to get the most money possible? If you would be willing to reconsider your decision about not selling the house, I would be willing to come take a look at the home and provide you with an update on the market. I'll give you an honest opinion about how you can net the most money possible. Would today or tomorrow work better for you?

Yes, I know you want to take a break. But you could lose money by doing that, can I explain? Just imagine that while you have it off the market, interest rates start to go up. It's a proven fact that when interest rates go up, the buyers dry up. Can you afford to take that chance, or would you want to list with an aggressive agent, like me, who can get your home sold?

Of course you are! Most people are really frustrated and disappointed when they have their house on the market for six months and it doesn't sell. That's clearly because you had an agent who dropped the ball. It's a little shocking to me because in the last six months I have sold over 20 homes, and I would have loved for yours to be one of them. Ultimately, you just want an agent who can sell your home, right?

෴

2.   I'm going to re-list with the same agent.

That sounds great! And let me ask you, have you ever had a chance to do something, and didn't do it? Has that ever happened to you? Well this time is just like that time, can I explain? Some agents only know one way to get a home sold. You know that now -- six months later, don't you? Or did you think that your agent was going to pull out their sure-fire-get-it-sold-quick plan after you were on the market for six long months? Clearly you see that you owe it to yourself to meet with me, so I can show you what I've done to get 20 homes sold in the last six months, or did you want your home to sit on the market for another six months?

That makes sense, and I'm curious, what specifically causes you to believe that six months wasn't more than enough time for the agent to get it sold the first time?

I appreciate that and what I am hearing you say is that you just want things to stay the way they are. Has there ever been a time when you kept doing things that same way and kept getting the same results? This time is just like that time, can I explain? The longer you stay with the same agent, the longer your house will be on the market. When you list with me, your house will go on the market as a new listing with a fresh, excited agent who will sell your house. Does that make sense?

Stop for a minute and consider how hiring an aggressive new agent might change the results you are getting. You can make a decision now whether you will stay with the same results, or hire an agent who has a track record of selling homes in 13 days. Can you see why it just makes sense to meet with me?

I can appreciate that you would consider giving this agent a second chance and yet I'm curious, do you think this agent will be able to do anything differently the next go round that they haven't already tried? Since you are considering re-listing, then obviously you feel they did everything they could to get the home sold. Doing the same thing again can't possibly create a different result, can it? Before you re-list, don't you think you owe it to yourself to get a second opinion before you tie yourself down for another six months?

You're going to re-list with the same agent, that's interesting. Is the agent a friend or something? If they couldn't get it sold in six months then I'm curious, what specifically causes you to believe that they will be able to sell it this time? I don't want to step on toes or anything like that, however since you obviously need to get the home sold I would like to interview with you and show you how I can help you. I have been able to sell 20 homes already this year and am confident that I can get your home sold as well. Why don't we get together today before you sign the paperwork with that agent and at least you'll have another opinion? I can stop by at two, or would four be better for you?

❦

3.　　I'm going to sell it myself.

I can appreciate that. You can cut your own hair, too, but would you?

I want you to meet with me, and I know you want to sell it yourself. But imagine for a moment that you meet with me, and find that I can get you what you want in a timely fashion that works for you and your family. Just like in the past when you've gotten good advice, and jumped on good opportunities, won't it be great to at least know you're making the right choice after meeting with me?

I can appreciate that you are thinking about selling it yourself. And I'm curious, why would you try it alone instead of hiring an active, aggressive agent, like me, who can actually get the home sold for you? Not all agents are created equal, and while your home was on the market I was able to sell 20 homes. Would you consider allowing me to interview with you to see if I can help you, before you spend your time marketing the home?

It makes sense that you would consider trying it on your own, since the home hasn't sold in six months. And let me ask you, if I could show you that I could get your home sold in the next 30 days and help you to move forward with your plans, would you consider meeting with me? Terrific! Would today or tomorrow be better for you?

Of course you want to sell it yourself because the other agent didn't do their job! That is exactly why you need an aggressive approach right now. Meet with me because I do what I say. Therefore, you won't be sitting here three months from now separated from your family. Would you even think about selling it yourself if you knew that you could hire me, net what you need, and be in your new house? Luckily, that's exactly why you had me out. Let's get started, ok?

I can appreciate that, what I am sensing is that you would like to have control over the process, is that correct? And because I can see that you do want some strong input into the process, we can work together on advertising, staging the home, and marketing to come to some agreement that will make you feel comfortable, okay?

Would you be willing to let an aggressive, active agent like me show you how I sell homes, or would you want to go ahead and list the house, get it sold quickly, and still feel confident that you have been well taken care of?

～

4.   I already have another agent in mind.

Of course you do! That's because you and I haven't met to discuss my track record and marketing plan for your home. When do you want to get together, today or tomorrow at three?

I understand. And let me ask you, do you just go to one dealership when looking to buy a car, or do you shop around for the best deal?

I can appreciate that. So, are you saying that a no obligation, fifteen minute meeting to find out if you've made the right choice would be a waste of time when selling your most valuable asset?

That's great that you have someone in mind. And since you will be signing a multi-month contract for thousands of dollars, it certainly couldn't hurt to get a second opinion could it?

I can appreciate that you have an agent in mind. And yet, don't you want to at least interview two agents to ensure that you are getting the best price, marketing plan, and service?

I understand that you have another agent in mind, and that's exactly why you should meet with me. I love competition and my job is to show you how I can put more dollars in your pocket than the other agent. So if there was even a chance that you could make more money with me, wouldn't it be worth 30 minutes of your time to meet with me?

I want you to interview me, and I appreciate that there were things you liked about the other agent. Just imagine for a minute that you met with me, and you were blown away by my aggressive plan to get homes sold. Because my listings only average fifteen days on the market, and sell for 99% of their asking price. Aren't those the kind of results you want?

∾

CALLING FSBO's

1.   I'm not interested in working with agents.

I understand. So are you saying that you don't want to get your home sold? Let me ask you, why would someone try to buy a For Sale By Owner when 99.9% of the entire inventory of homes for sale is available for a free look with a real estate agent? You already know they're bargain hunting. So, you can fall prey to the vultures who want to pick at your equity like a dead carcass, or you can meet with an agent, like me, whose legal obligation is to protect your equity. Which is better for you?

I wouldn't be interested in working with agents either if I were you. I work with them every day and I feel the same! Unfortunately, virtually the entire inventory and, therefore, all of the buyers come through agents. So, not using agents is kind of like shooting yourself in the foot. I have an idea. Why don't you meet with me and find out that I clearly have your best interest at heart? That way, I can deal with all the other agents, and you won't have to. Won't that be great?

I can appreciate that you are going to sell it on your own. And I'm curious, if there were a way that I could net you the same amount of money that you're looking to net on your own, yet handle the sale for you, and get your home exposed to all the buyers in the market place, would you consider meeting with me to see if I can help you?

I understand that you don't want to work with agents. And are you aware that only 2% of For Sale By Owner's actually sell the home on their own? Can you afford only a 2% chance of selling the home, or did you want to guarantee the sale? Having already sold 20 homes this year, I am confident that I can sell the home. Why don't we get together today or tomorrow, and let me show you exactly how I can help you?

I hear what you're saying. And I'm curious; did you have a bad experience with an agent? Tell me about that. Would you agree that an agent with my experience might do something differently than an agent who is brand new, or only sells a few homes a year?

I understand. So let me ask you a question, have you ever been fishing? Selling yourself is like fishing in one fishing hole with one kind of bait. While you might catch a fish, I have lots of fishing holes and all kinds of bait. So my odds of catching a fish sooner are much better.

～

2.   I already have an agent in mind.

Really? Which agent are you planning to list with? That's interesting, and how did you happen to choose that agent? Since this is obviously a big decision for you, and you will be signing a multi-month contract for thousands of dollars, would you consider getting a second opinion to make sure that you are getting the best price, marketing plan and service? Because if you would be willing to get a second opinion, I would be willing to meet with you and show you exactly how I've been able to sell 50 homes already this year.

You already have an agent in mind? That's great, and I want you to set an appointment with me so I can give you a second opinion on everything to ensure that you are making the very best decision possible. A second opinion never hurts, does it? Great! I can stop by today or tomorrow at four. Which works best for you?

I understand. And so how come you haven't listed with them yet? Can I tell you why that concerns me? That agent is content to wait and let you call them after you get frustrated from not selling. As professional agents, we know that you will statistically sell for less money than if listed. So since that agent is doing you a disservice by letting you try to sell it yourself, do you want to make more or less money? Then let's meet to get you more money. Does today or tomorrow work better for you?

That makes sense. And since you went using no realtor whatsoever to keying in on one of the 1500 in the market, should I assume that agent completely blew you away with how good they are, or would it benefit you to get a second opinion before you take a giant leap of faith?

Does that agent have a track record of selling homes in fourteen days? Because that's exactly what I've done for my clients this year. Most typical agents average 68 days on the market before their listings sell. So, if I could get your home sold and save you time and money with a real aggressive plan, wouldn't it make sense to meet with me and hear what I have to say?

Of course you do, and that's not a problem. Just talking with you today verifies that you like to have choices so you can make the best decision, is that true? The great thing about this process is that you're in the driver's seat and you already said you need to be moved in one month. Clearly you need someone who can be really aggressive about the marketing of this house so that you can get your money out and be in the new house. Isn't that what you want?

∽

3.   Bring me a buyer and I'll pay you a commission.

I appreciate your offer to pay me a 3% commission. And may I tell you what concerns me about this in considering your best interest? You are actually offering thousands of dollars to an agent to negotiate against you and look out for the buyer's best interests, while leaving yourself vulnerable and unprotected. Did you want to pay an agent to negotiate against you? Tell you what, it could be possible that I can net you the same amount of money that you are looking to net on your own, yet handle the sale for you and get your home exposed to all the buyers in the marketplace. If I can show you a way to do this, would you consider hiring me? Great! I can come by today or tomorrow at four, which would work best for you?

Thank you for offering me 3%, I will mention that to my buyers agent in case she is working with anyone that your home could be of interest to. I personally focus 100% of my time on servicing my sellers and getting my listings sold. Since you are already prepared to pay 3%, it's very possible that I could handle the sale for you and net you the same amount of money that you are looking to net on your own. If I can do this for you, would you allow me to list your home?

You can do it that way and maybe attract a few more buyers to the house. That would work if there was no inventory on the market right now, but you have seen that the market is flooded with listings, haven't you? So buyers have lots of options, and most agents won't even bother to show your house if it's not listed. Your house may never sell if it's not exposed to the entire market. You can continue like this, trying to attract a few buyers at a time or you can meet with me and I will get you moved with the most money in your pocket. What day works best for you?

Thank you, that's great. Let me ask you a question, because I have a concern about that. It's a great strategy to attract agents who will tell you they have a buyer when they just want to get their foot in the door. I would rather be very honest with you, and tell you that I am calling to show you how I have netted the most money for my sellers. Is there any reason you would not meet with me if I could show you my proven track record for aggressively marketing the home and getting you more money?

That's a great idea, and has anyone taken you up on it? Can I tell you why I think that might be happening? Did you know that in this market the average agent sells just four homes a year? And with the average commission being $4,000, that's an annual income of only $16,000 a year. So clearly that makes for a lot of desperate agents, right? Let me ask you, as a business person, if you were desperate and had someone in your car that represented one fourth of your total yearly income, would you take them to see homes that are listed where the commission is guaranteed, or would you take them to a For Sale By Owner where there's no guarantee?

Thank you for the offer! So let me get this straight, you're offering me 3% and you want to save the other 3%, right? Ok, great, and I'm curious. After you pay for your own advertising, disrupt your family time showing your house at all hours, host your own open houses every weekend, negotiate with low-balling, bargain-hunting buyers, if any actually make an offer, and then finally pay lawyer fees, will you really be saving anything, and if so, will it really be worth it?

☙

4.   If it doesn't sell on my own, I just won't sell.

I understand but you really don't want to spend another winter in Pennsylvania, do you? Imagine for a moment that together we stage your home to get the highest possible price and get you to Florida. And, just like you've done in the past when you needed help, you got the right person. So when you arrive in Florida with all of your equity, won't you be glad you didn't just give up?

So, let me ask you, what specifically causes you to believe that there is only one way to sell your house? You want to sell the house yourself, but you are saying that if that the one method doesn't work you are not willing to look at other options. Not only could you list with an agent like me, you could go to auction, you could rent it, or you could look at what will net you the most money. Before you make a major decision, wouldn't you want to know what all the options are, especially if there is a chance you could make more? When is the best time for us to meet, Tuesday or Thursday?

Of course you would feel that way because you are trying net the most money in your pocket and avoid paying a big commission, aren't you? Imagine for a moment, that I could help you get exactly what you need out of this house, get it sold for you, and create a pleasurable experience for you along the way. If I could make all this happen, would you consider allowing me to assist you?

I understand. And I'm curious, what's stopping you from hiring an agent that can help you get the home sold and get you to your new place? I have helped many folks just like you, who first tried For Sale By Owner. They listed the home with me, and I was able to net them much more than they ever thought possible while taking care of everything for them. Would it be worth 20 minutes of your time to see if I can do the same thing for you before you give up on what you really want?

I can appreciate that, and let's see if we can make this work for you, ok? You're obviously selling it yourself to save money, right? And you do want to move, correct? Ok, so what if I could get you sold <u>and</u> save that money for you? Would it be worth fifteen minutes of your time to find out how?

Would you stop and look at how you could be cutting off your nose to spite your face? Selling a home on your own is statistically one of the hardest business transactions you can attempt to pull off. And most people who do it end up getting less money anyway. Why don't we get together so that I can help you sell your home and make <u>more</u> money? Does today or tomorrow work better for you?

5.   I'm going to continue on my own for now.

I understand that you want to continue on your own. And has there ever been a time that you tried to do something yourself and regretted it? That time is just like this time, can I explain? The more you struggle selling this on your own, the more you will understand why you should hire me to get the job done. Hiring me simply means that you will have the best outcome, isn't that what you want?

I can appreciate that. I'm curious, what specifically causes you to believe that you will have a smooth settlement if you sell it yourself? The more you expose yourself to liability, the more you will want a professional to handle it for you. And using a professional like me, who is aware of all the legal and customary practices, simply means that you will get to the settlement table. So would you want to try to learn real estate law overnight or would you rather just get the house sold?

I understand that you want to continue on your own for now. And imagine for a moment that we set an appointment, and I show you a way that I could net you the same amount of money you're looking to net on your own, yet I could handle the sale for you and get your home exposed to all the buyers in the market, and potentially do it much faster than you can on your own, wouldn't that be great?

I can appreciate that you want to continue on your own for now, and yet week after week the home is sitting on the market not selling. You do want to be sold don't you? I want you to meet with me, so I can show you how I can help you get the home sold, and not have it become one of those homes that is shopworn by being on the market for so long. You do realize the longer the home is on the market the harder it becomes to sell, don't you?

That makes sense and what's important about selling it on your own? So, if you found out that I could net you the same or more money and do all the work for you, would that be a benefit to you?

Sounds good. And let me ask you, when you're driving and you realize that you're lost, do you keep driving down the same road you're on, or do you turn around and go a different direction? Good, so let's get together and turn this around from for sale to sold!

ꝏ

6.   If I list, it will be with a discount broker.

I can see why you would consider listing with a discount broker and what I really hear you saying is that you want to ensure the most money in your pocket, am I correct? So may I share some statistics with you? The average list to sale price ratio of those discount brokers is only 93% while mine is 99%. This means I am actually going to net you more money in the end. And since selling a home in today's market is such a challenge, can you really afford to have a discounted service or did you want to guarantee the sale?

Naturally you would consider hiring a discount broker to save on the commission. And let me ask you, has there ever been a time when you tried to go the cheaper route and in the end you found that it actually cost you more than if you had gone the other way? Well this time is just like that time may I explain? Listing with a discount broker gives you much less exposure and service than listing with a full time professional like me. And their list to sale price ratio is actually way less than mine, which means they may actually cost you money in the end? Would it be worth your time to check out a different option before going the cheapest route?

Yes, you could do that, but if you look up the definition of "discount" in the dictionary it says, "Discount is the amount a price would be reduced to purchase a product of lesser grade." In other words you get what you pay for! You can list with a discount broker and get an agent of lesser grade, or you can pay a full commission and get an agent who is skilled in selling homes for top dollar. Which would you prefer?

Don't list with a discount broker unless you want to lose money. Listing with a discount broker is like hiring a car salesman to sell your house. They wheel and deal and discount your house to move it, that's not what you want, is it? There is a reason why over 60 sellers a year pay me a full commission to get them top dollar and get them moved. They appreciate that I protect their equity like a guard dog. So of course you can list with a discount broker, or you can list with a professional with a mindset of doing whatever it takes to get you top dollar. And that's really what you want, isn't it?

Why? Do you have a discount house?

I understand. And let me ask you, if you needed a doctor would you go with the cheapest doctor or the best doctor? Then how come when it comes to selling what's possibly your most valuable asset you want to go with the cheapest?

It makes total sense that you want to use a discount broker and save money. And let me ask you, if it really worked, wouldn't everyone be doing it? I mean, wouldn't I be out of business instead of helping 20 people sell their homes this year? The truth is that discount brokers know the public likes to think they can save money, that's their hook. Really, if it wasn't for the thought of a discount, would you honestly be thinking of hiring that agent?

∾

7.   I can do the same things that you do.

I can see your point, when you consider what most agents do to sell homes. I'm curious, are you familiar with my system for selling homes? What would be the best time to show you? Statistics show that agents in our area only sell two homes per year, on average, and I've already sold 20 homes so far. So that proves I have something a little different to offer, don't you agree?

I can appreciate that. What I hear you saying is that you don't think agents do much to sell homes, am I right? Let me ask you, if I could show you an active and aggressive marketing plan with a proven track record to get your home sold, would you consider hiring me?

I understand totally, we live in a do it yourself world. People, like yourself can put a sign in the yard, advertise and put the house on the internet. Here is my concern; how many buyers do you know who are looking for a house right now? I have a database of buyers that I match with properties every day. Can you see the advantage of using an agent who has those kinds of connections?

You probably could do some of the same things. But let's go over my marketing plan and I'll show you the 50 action items that I will be doing to sell your home. Will you have time to do all these, or just a few? You might have to cut back on your hours at work to do all this! If you really want to buy the other property, then we need to move quickly to get this home sold and get you into the house you want. You could do some of the same things, but why delay the sale of your house?

Really? You can get ten homes sold in three months for 98% of the asking price in an average of 25 days? My broker is going to call you because we could use some good agents like yourself!

Of course you think that you can do what I do. I haven't shown you any of the mounds of legal paperwork, how to deal with tire kicking buyers, or how to pre-qualify them when it comes to selling a house. No wonder you think that! When you see all that's involved in not only selling but safely getting to closing, you'll naturally want to meet with me. What's good for you today or tomorrow?

☙

8.   I've done it myself before.

I did it myself too; a long, long time ago. How long ago did you sell your last house? Ten years ago? Good for you! And I have to tell you that the real estate market has really changed since then; the paperwork alone is monumental. We have disclosures out the ying-yang, and the standard contract is about 16 pages. Most buyers get a little uncomfortable when they work directly with a seller and all this paperwork is coming at them. Can you imagine how intimidating that is? Yes, it's not like the old days and most buyers will actually avoid you. You can't afford to let that happen, can you?

That doesn't surprise me because you obviously have been closely following the market and have a lot of knowledge about this. And I'm sure you already know it's a verifiable fact that most sellers use an agent to sell their home. And because 95% of all properties are listed with an agent, 95% of all buyers buy something that's listed. That only leaves 5% for you. If you played that in Vegas, it wouldn't be very good odds in today's market, would it?

Congratulations! You were one of the lucky ones. Do you know that only 2% of For Sale By Owner's actually sell themselves? And of those, they typically get up to 27% less than homes listed with an agent. Did you have to negotiate down the last time you sold? Frankly, it sounds like you were the exception to the rule. Why don't we do this, let's get together and put a solid plan of action in place to get you sold and not take any chances, shouldn't you?

I'm sure you have, and was it more than 5 years ago? Then you know the market has changed tremendously, and there are so many new legal developments as well. What it took to sell a house just a few years ago won't get the job done today. Why don't we get together so that I can help you get it sold in today's market, isn't that what you want?

That's fantastic that you've done it on your own before, and may I ask you a really important question? Was the market as flat as it is now? Then undoubtedly you can see the value in having a true full time professional working on your behalf to ensure that the home actually sells. And you do want the most money possible for the home, don't you?

That's great that you were able to do it on your own before. With the market being as challenging as it is, do you think you'll be able to do it again this time and actually save money? I want you to meet with me so I can clearly show you where you compare in the market right now. Then together we can crunch the numbers to see if there is a possibility of my helping you. I'll get your home exposed to all the buyers in the marketplace and get you the most money possible, isn't that what you want?

∽

9.   If we don't sell it, we'll rent it.

You could rent it, but what about capital gains? You should really check with your accountant. Renting it could cause you to lose money because the tax status of the property will change. You could sell it now, and owe no capital gains, or rent it and when you do decide to sell it pay thousands in taxes. That's not good, is it?

Stop and think about what it will mean to rent the house out. You might get a renter that really ruins what you have here, I've seen it happen. Renters don't respect a house the way the owners do, that's a given. So think about how you might actually lose money by renting it, because it will never show as well as it does now, will it?

I understand that renting is an option for you, and yet you have the home for sale for a reason, right? So even though you could rent, what you're saying is that you would definitely rather sell the home, wouldn't you? Ok, great! Let's get together at no obligation or expense, and see if I can help you get all this taken care of in a way that works for you, okay?

Of course you can rent the home. And while the market doesn't seem to be getting better, wouldn't you rather sell now to ensure the most money in your pocket? Or would you rather have to do repairs and improvements, especially after a tenant trashes your house?

I understand, and do you really want to be a landlord? I know it's frustrating right now, and can you imagine the frustration of chasing down a tenant for late rent, month after month, getting repair calls in the middle of the night, and just generally being chained to this house for a year at a time? Don't you just want to get it sold?

I can appreciate that. And why would you want to get involved in something as complicated as being a landlord, when you just wanted to sell it in the first place? It may seem like a way to make or save money now, but you're on the hook for the mortgage and taxes every month, regardless of if the tenant pays or not. And what if they break the lease? You're left holding the bag. And, let's not even go into tenant insurance, repairs, etc. Why don't we simply get together so I can help you get the home sold, isn't that what you want?

◌

SETTING THE APPOINTMENT

1.   I used to have my license.

I can appreciate that. What I am sensing is that you want to have control over the process, is that correct? And because I can see that you want some strong input, we can work together on advertising, staging the home, and marketing to come to some agreements that will make you feel comfortable. Or would you want to just go ahead and list the house, get it sold quickly, and feel like you've been well taken care of?

That's great! Then you already know that all agents are <u>not</u> the same, right? You've been there; most agents hang around the office and drink coffee! And if you'd be willing to meet with me, I'd be willing to answer any questions, and work with you on what <u>you</u> want and get the home sold, sound fair?

Oh great! So you know first hand how hard I'm going to work to get your home sold. I can't wait to meet with you and talk shop. What's the best time to come over and show you my marketing plan, four or five?

You did? That's perfect, because now you'll definitely appreciate my marketing plan and approach for getting your home sold. Since you already know exactly what works and what doesn't you'll love what I'm going to do for you. I'm so excited to share it with you! When would be a good time for you today or tomorrow?

Terrific! And how long ago was that? Then I'm sure I don't have to tell you that the paperwork, disclosures and process in general has changed many times over since then. It has become almost monumental just to get a deal closed. Surely you want a full time professional looking out for you on all that, especially since you already understand the importance of it all, don't you?

Having had your license before means I definitely don't have to tell you why it's so important for you to hire an agent to protect your equity and interest, do I? I bet you are just searching for an agent who is worthy of paying, aren't you? I would like to apply for the job. What would be a good time for me to meet with you to show you exactly how I can help you get the most money possible, and take care of your best interests?

❧

2.   We want to do some work before we put it on the market.

So what I am hearing you say is that you want your house to show in the very best light, and I do, too! So let's do this, let's make a list of the things that will absolutely affect the price, and set a date you can have them done. I've seen time and time again things will get done quicker and easier if we set a deadline to get the house on the market. As a matter of fact, I'd recommend that we sign the contract tonight and postdate it so that date is very real in your mind. Does that make sense?

Yes, you can do some work on the house and you can lose money doing it, can I explain? We have a good picture of the market right now, but we don't know what it will look like 30 days from now. You could miss ten to twelve buyers and lose money if the market goes down, which, in all likelihood, it will. Can you afford to spend the time taking several weeks to work on the house and have the value drop by several thousand dollars?

Ouch! Can I tell you why that might be the worse thing you could do? It's been proven that sellers maybe get 50 cents on every dollar they spend to fix up or upgrade. And nine out of ten times the work takes longer than you expect. So, as your home sits off the market for weeks or months, missing potential buyer after buyer, all you get is the privilege of spending $10,000 to make $5,000. Is that what you want?

I understand. And I'm curious; do you really think that a buyer is going to give you dollar for dollar what you pay to fix up his or her new house?

That sounds valid. And let me ask you, if you were a buyer would you want a house at $250,000 that needed some work, and is priced right, or would you want to pay $260,000 knowing that the seller just did $10,000 worth of work that you may not even like?

Perfect! Let's go ahead and sign the contract tonight. We'll make a list of all the things you will be doing to the home. We can either let all potential buyers and other agents know exactly what you are planning to do, or we can have the home formally go on the market as soon as the work is done. This way we can start the marketing campaign right away and get the home sold as soon as possible, okay?

Let me ask you, are you looking to do this work to get more money out of the house, or to have the home show better? I want you to meet with me so I can help you decide what things are going to benefit you. It could be that some of what you are thinking about doing is not actually going to get you more money. Let's meet today or tomorrow so I can make sure you're doing the things that will actually make a difference for you. We can go ahead and sign the paperwork so I can get started with marketing while you're finishing up the work. That way, as soon as you're done, we'll start showing the home, okay?

~

3. I want to find the right house before I list mine.

Can I tell you about what happened to some other buyers who found their dream house before they had their house listed? They found a house they absolutely fell in love with and <u>they lost it</u> because their house wasn't sold, and the sellers would not look at a contingent offer. They were heartbroken! Scott and Christy, I don't want to see that happen to you. There is another way we can do this: list your house tonight and we will make it contingent on you finding suitable housing. Isn't that better?

We can find you the right house, but are you willing to have two mortgages? If you are, that's great! We'll pull an additional loan on your house to put down on the other house, and you will have three payments until your house sells. Would having two mortgages be comfortable for you?

Terrific! And let me ask you, can you purchase the house without selling yours first, or do you need to sell your home before buying? You are going to have much more negotiating power to get the best deal on the next house if your home is already sold, as opposed to not even being listed on the market. As a seller, would you be most willing to negotiate with a buyer whose house isn't even on the market yet?

You do? Why? You said you can't buy anything before yours sells, so why would we find the perfect house for you and then risk losing it after you get your heart set on it? And you do want to get the best deal on the next house, don't you? Well, let me ask you something. Let's say you're a seller and you have a choice. One choice is to accept an offer contingent up on the sale of a house that isn't even on the market. The other choice is an offer where the house is already on the market and priced right, getting lots of showings. In which scenario would you be more willing to negotiate?

I felt the same way, and then I realized that sellers today aren't even entertaining offers from buyers that don't have their home already on the market. Really, looking for a house without yours sold, or even on the market is putting the cart before the horse, does that make sense?

I understand how you feel. And I just want you to imagine what it would feel like to lose the house of your dreams because you found it and then had to put your old home on the market to keep the new one. Or, you had to list your old home way below market value to ensure a quick sale. You don't want that, do you?

∽

4.   We already talked to someone from your company.

That's great! I want you to get all the opinions you can so you can feel comfortable that you are making the right decision. Here's what is going to happen. You will interview several agents and one will stand out who will do the best job for you, isn't that what you want? So what would be best for you, Tuesday or Thursday?

Great! Since it's not the company that actually sells the home, or really has anything at all to do with the process, naturally you can sell how it just makes sense to interview me. This way I can provide you with a second opinion on everything, okay? And since not all agents are created equal, undoubtedly you'll want to get the most active and aggressive agent with proven results, don't you? Let's get together today at four or six, which works best for you?

I'm sure you have. I'm sorry you weren't impressed with that other agent. And did you know that each agent is an independent contractor? We all basically run our own business and work for our clients. What's the best time to come over and show you how I'm going to <u>work for you</u> to get you top dollar for your home?

∽

5.   Send me your card and I'll call you.

Definitely, I understand! What I sense is you don't want to be pressured into a decision until you are ready, right? I feel the same way about pressure. So, if you knew I would give you the time to feel comfortable about your decision, could we meet and I will explain everything?

You are probably getting lots of calls, aren't you? And the more you think about it, the more you will be convinced that I am the agent to get the job done. You do want an agent who can get your home sold, don't you? What would be best for you, four o'clock today or tomorrow?

I will definitely send you my card. And since you obviously still want to sell the home, we could easily get together this afternoon for 15 or 20 minutes. I can meet you in person and show you exactly how I've sold 20 homes while yours was on the market. Does three or four today work for you?

I can send you my card and follow up with you in a few days. And since it sounds like you really need to sell the home, I want to meet with you right away so you won't lose anymore valuable marketing time. I'm sure you already sense that my approach, sales skills and communications are quite different from other agents who've called you, can't you? I promise that if you meet with me for only a few minutes, you'll come away with all the information you'll need to help you make the right decision for yourself, okay?

That sounds great! And do you want an agent who simply sends you mail and waits by the phone, or a professional agent who demonstrates good sales skills by setting an appointment while you're trying to get him off the phone?

Ok, I will. And what's the best time for us to get together so I can help you sell your home?

Certainly! In fact, why don't I just come over and hand deliver it to you. What's the best time today, two o'clock or four?

༄

AT THE LISTING APPOINTMENT

1. We'll think it over and get back to you.

Of course you do! After all, this is a big decision for you. And since I do this day in and day out for hundreds of families year after year, let's think this through together now to ensure that you are making the right decision, okay?

I get that this is a big decision for you, and you need to make sure you are comfortable with your choice of agents. Just so I'm clear, what specifically is holding you back from hiring me tonight? Perfect. Let me ask you, are you as confident as I am that I can get your home sold? Great! Let's go ahead and sign the contract so I can get started for you tomorrow, okay?

I can appreciate that you would want to think it over. Why don't we go ahead and sign the contract, and I'll leave it with you to think over tonight? Then I can pick it up in the morning when I bring the sign and lockbox. Does that work for you?

Do you feel that I can get your home sold? Sounds like it would make you more comfortable to talk between yourselves for a few minutes, right? I've got a few phone calls to return, so let me go out on the porch and I will be back in fifteen minutes. If you still have questions, I will be happy to answer them and we will get the home sold together. How does that sound?

I can appreciate that. And what I am sensing is you're worried that you might make the wrong choice, is that correct? I get that, so let's go down the contract and I will explain everything to you, from how we will stage the house, to how we'll position it to get you top dollar. And if you feel comfortable after that discussion, then we'll get the house on the market first thing in the morning, sound good?

Naturally, because I really wasn't as strong as I could've been in my presentation to show you how aggressively I'm going to market your home. So, what I'm going to do is ask you to sign the contract again. And as you do, you'll be totally confident that I'm going to get you the most money for your home and protect your equity like a guard dog. Do you want top dollar?

Of course you want to think it over. That's because you have some unanswered questions that I didn't cover for you. So, go ahead, ask me what you need to ask me so you can make your decision.

❦

2.   We have a couple of other agents to interview.

And you should pick the right agent for the job! If you knew that I outperform the market by getting my sellers 99% of their asking price, then you would feel comfortable that you don't even need to talk to the other agents, right?

And you can interview them. As a matter of fact, there are 1000 agents in this market and you could interview all of them and just be 1000 times more convinced that I am the right agent to list your house! Ultimately it's not your job to entertain agents; it's your job to find the right agent. So, Scott and Christy, do you think that I can sell your home?

Okay, you have other agents to interview. And after all that we just discussed, is there something that you are not comfortable with, or something that you feel is missing? Because I certainly feel confident that I can sell your home, and I want you to list with me now so I can get started first thing tomorrow! I would be happy to cancel the appointments for you. I mean, after all, this will give you more time to enjoy your family while you trust the sale of the house to me, okay?

You have other agents to interview? Hmmm, I'm curious. What specifically causes you to believe that you will find a better agent out there? I mean the average agent here only sells four homes all year and I've shown you that I've already sold 30 homes this year. Plus, I have a higher list to sale price ratio and less days on market than the average. Aren't you looking for results?

I can appreciate that, and that doesn't work for me, or for you. What kind of a salesperson would I be if I just walked out that door and hoped you liked me enough to call me after you're done talking to other agents? The stronger I appear to be now, the stronger I'll be when negotiating an offer for your home. You want a strong agent who can get you top dollar for your house, right? Good, let's sign the contract so I can do that for you, and I'll give the other agents first shot at bringing a buyer, okay?

Wow, I am so sorry. I should've let you know that I needed to be the last agent you'd interview. My track record clearly shows why you would choose me to sell your home. But until you interview those other agents, you won't know that. So let's do this: I don't want to pressure you into signing now when you obviously need to talk to the other agents. Let me help you with the questions you need to ask them, and the answers that they should give. Then you can see what I mean, and that way I can come back after you're done and we can get you on the market and sold. When's your last interview?

༄

3.   The other agent agreed to do it for less commission.

It's great that the other agent said they will do it for less. And I'm curious; did that agent share with you what their current list to sale price ratio is? And did they also share their track record of how many homes they've actually sold versus just listed? The reason I ask you this is because it doesn't really matter what commission they charge if they can't actually get it sold. Does that make sense?

I can appreciate that the other agent has offered to do it for less. And I'm curious; do you know how many listings that agent actually has right now? My concern is that they may just be trying to get a listing and, in turn, be able to use your home to pick up other deals. I have ten listings right now, and my intention is to help you actually get the home sold, and not just take a listing. That is what you want, isn't it?

That would be great if the agent could actually provide you with the same service for less, but they can't! I have a question for you: why would an agent work for less? Could it be because they are desperate for business? And if they are desperate for your business, chances are they don't have the skills to keep their own business going, let alone manage your biggest financial investment. Doesn't it just make sense to hire an expert in the field to protect your equity?

So can I ask you, do you want an agent who will get you less for your house?

That sounds great, and did they tell you how they're really going to save you that commission? There are only a couple places it can come from, can I explain? To justify cutting their commission, they will either have to provide less service and marketing, or they will have to entice every other agent in town to bring a buyer. And the only way to entice an agent to come to a cut commission property is to let them know that they can bring virtually any low offer. Do either of those things sound like they will work in your favor?

That makes sense. And would you be interested in how I can make you more money? It's simple math really. The agent who said they will do it for 5% is going to get you about 91% of your asking price, as you can see by these market stats. And, as you can clearly see by my track record, I'm averaging 98% of asking price. So, you obviously get what you pay for. By paying 6% and listing with me I make you, on average, 7% more money than that other agent. That's a 6% net to you, or $18,000 more in your pocket. Could you use an extra $18,000?

∿

4.   We only want to list for 90 days.

Our policy is no less than six months. But if you commit to me tonight, I will list it for 90 days with an automatic 30 day extension, that is, if you are happy with what we are doing. Does that make sense?

As we look at the numbers together, the average house is on the market for 100 days, or more. So, can you tell me what's important about only listing for 90 days? Is it because you simply want to get the home sold as fast as possible for the most money? Well I want that too, and our standard listing agreement is six months. List with me and I will do everything I can to get this home sold quickly, and if you are not satisfied with the level of service and enthusiasm I am giving this process, you can let me know at any time. Is that fair?

I tell you what, lets list it for the six month period that I require. I'll offer you a risk free guarantee in writing that will allow you to cancel our agreement at anytime, with no strings attached, if you are unhappy with what I'm doing to sell your home, okay?

I understand. So are you saying you don't want to sell the home? The average time on the market for a home is 5 ½ months, so what benefit do you think you will get by listing it for only three?

That's valid. And let me ask you, would you tell your lawyer she can take your case but she only has ninety days, then you'll switch lawyers? Of course you wouldn't, and lawyers bill you for their time! Clearly you know that when you hire a professional, like me, I'm going to want to do the job as fast as possible for you. I only get paid when you get paid. And I don't know about you, but I'd like to be paid sooner rather than later. How about you?

That makes sense, and why don't we do this? Sign a listing for six months, and I'll write in that you have the right to cancel after 90 days if you're not satisfied, okay?

೦ಾ

5.   We want lots of open houses.

We could do open houses, it's just like throwing a party for the neighbors because that's typically who shows up.

Remember when we listed the house and I told you it was by appointment only? That's because we want to honor your time with qualified, pre-approved buyers. Do you want this to be like a car dealership where we throw open the doors and everyone tromps through with no intention of buying? And while it might seem like you have more activity that way, it's really not bringing you a good solid motivated buyer who will write a contract. Are you seeing that?

You want lots of open houses. I can understand why you would think doing open houses is what sells homes, since that's all most agents know how to do and you see them doing them left and right. And yet, it has been proven that less than 1% of homes actually sell as a direct result of an open house. While 90% of the listings I take sell from my marketing efforts. Which is better for you 1% or 90%?

Open houses used to be one of the few ways to get a home sold, and in today's market and society, it really isn't safe. Imagine for a moment that we open your house up to any stranger that wants to walk in, and I have more than a few people here at once. How can I possibly watch your belongings and ensure that its all protected? Besides less than 1% of homes are sold as a direct result of an open house anyway. Let's take the more active and aggressive approach and get the home sold, okay?

I could do them for you, but are you looking to get your home sold or simply give me leads? Open houses are great for new agents to get some potential leads that might buy in three to six months. They don't sell the home, however. So if you want to go away every weekend, you'd be doing some new agents in my office a favor. But, I'm afraid you'd only be inconveniencing yourselves. You don't want that, do you?

Everyone's heard that open houses are a good marketing tool, and really it's like going fishing without any bait. If you're really, really lucky, you might catch a fish that happens to run into your hook. But for the most part you're just going to be frustrated, waiting around for nothing. Tell you what, let me put my proven marketing plan to work for you and get your home sold quickly. Isn't that what you want?

༄

6.   The other agent said they could get us a higher price.

Wow, it really concerns me that they would tell you that, may I tell you why? Well agents are not actually the ones to determine the price, the market is. And can you see that the market isn't justifying a higher price if you want to be sold? I'm afraid that this agent is either to weak to stand up to you and tell you the truth because its not what you really want to hear, or they just want to use your listing as a tool to pick up business for themselves. You want a strong agent that can tell you the truth and get your home sold, don't you?

I can see that the other agent would tell you that because most of them are afraid to tell the truth. It takes being quite strong to tell you the truth when you stand to lose a listing, does that make sense? I'm not looking to just take another listing, what I'm looking to do is be honest with you, straight forward and tell you what I feel it will take to actually get your home sold, and not just listed like the other thousands of homes that are for sale right now.

Of course they said they could get you a higher price, because that's exactly what some agents do. It's called "buying" the listing. They tell you a price that's high so you'll list with them. I have one job to do and that's to make sure you get your home sold in the time that you want. And if you want that to happen we need to pick a price together that will cause offers to come in. So, you can list with an agent who is just telling you what you want to hear, and the house will take forever to sell, or you can list with an agent who is honest with you and will get the home sold. Which would you prefer?

I think you already know which agent is telling you the truth and trying to make sure you get moved. And I don't blame you for wanting to believe the other agent. Who wouldn't want to believe they can get more than the market will bear? The numbers speak for themselves when you look at the comparative market analysis and see what has actually sold. You can hope for a higher price, but unless that agent has a magic wand we need to stick with what's right here in black and white. So, what price will you list your home for tonight?

First of all, I want you to know something. This is your house and you can price it at whatever you want, right? And yet, I get really concerned when I hear that an agent might come in and just tell you what you want to hear in order to get the listing. I mean we can list it higher, but does it really seem like that's what the market will give us when it comes right down to it? I definitely want to work with you on this, but I also want to tell you truth. Isn't that the kind of agent you want in your corner?

Perfect! Would you take my calculator and multiply that agent's price by the market average list to sale ratio of 91%? Okay, now please write down that number. Now, take my suggested list price and multiply it by 98%. Which number is bigger?

I can see how that would be enticing, and I have one question. You've just seen the data that supports $289,900, so why would even give a second thought to someone who's not even as smart as you when it comes to knowing the market?

∽

7.   We want to list high and come down later.

That makes sense that you would want to start out high to leave room for negotiating, and may I tell you why that concerns me? Well, the first thirty days is generally when you get the most interest and activity on the house. And if we price it too high we could miss out on a lot of buyers.

Since we will never get a second chance to make the first impression on the market, wouldn't it be better to get the most exposure the first time around? Let's go ahead and list at $199,900 and get the home maximum exposure. That is what you want, right?

Don't list high unless you want to sit on the market month after month with no activity. In today's market, serious buyers won't even bother to look at properties that are overpriced, because they have way too much to choose from. You don't want to be overlooked by the serious buyers do you? Great lets list at a price that will cause the home to sell, okay?

No problem, listing higher simply means the house will be on the market longer, is that okay with you? We'll just extend the listing to a year, okay?

Without exception, we see that when people list high their house is on the market 30% to 50% longer. So the average house is on the market right now for 90 days and listing it high means your house could be on the market for six months or longer. That means you will have double payments eating up your equity as well as yard maintenance, utility bills, cleaning, and checking on the property. We also see when houses are listed at market value offers come in faster and closer to the asking price, which sometimes means multiple offers. Now that would be pretty sweet, wouldn't it?

That makes sense. And I'm curious, what specifically causes you to believe that anyone will even look at a property that's over priced?

I want you to list at $299,900, and I know you want to list it at $325,000. But imagine for a moment that you're sitting here, in the same house six months later, wondering why no one even bothered to make an offer.

⁓

8.   We want you to cut your commission.

You know I totally understand that you want me to cut my commission, and if I were you I would want that, too. But the fact is, you need to sell the home don't you? And I have to tell you, the weaker an agent is with you on their commission, the weaker they will be when it comes time to negotiate your price. You don't want a weak agent negotiating on your behalf do you? Good, let's sign the contract so I can get your price.

It makes sense that you don't want to pay full commission, and almost everyone selling a home feels just like you do. Let me ask you; is your home one of the largest investments that you own? So you want to ensure that your best interests are protected, and that you get the most money possible in the end, don't you? Well how strong is an agent, who can't even stand up to you for their own worth, able to protect your equity? I understand, and let's go ahead and sign the contract so I can take care of you, okay?

I get it; you don't want to pay a full commission. That's a pretty typical concern because you think it will cost you something, right? What if I could prove to you beyond a shadow of a doubt that buyers will pay more for your house when it's listed, and you will net more in your pocket? Would there be any reason not to list if that was the case?

Would you agree that most sellers are pretty value conscious, just like you? And don't you think that if they could make more money by not paying a full commission,

<u>everyone</u> would do it? And yet most people who are selling a house pick a top agent, like me, to net them more money in their pocket. Can I show you how?

I can appreciate that. And since you've seen everything I'm going to do to get your home sold for an average of 5% more than any other agent in this market, what services would you like me to cut so that I can afford to work for the lower commission?

I know it sounds good, but what you're doing is telling every agent right from the start that you are taking money out of their pocket. How enthusiastic do you think they'll be to show your home versus the other homes that pay higher commission?

∾

9.   Since we're also buying with you, will you reduce your commission?

I certainly know that you want to save money, let me ask you a question. Have you ever been asked to take a pay cut at work on an important job? Well that's what you are asking me to do. You see, I coordinate this all the time and there are a lot of details involved that you won't even appreciate till we get right down to the end. So, when we are sitting at the settlement table and I have put all the money in your pocket you deserve, you'll be pretty happy, right?

Yes, I can't reduce my commission and I want you to get the best service. I want to give you all of my efforts to get your home sold and find the right house for you to purchase. In fact, that's exactly why you should trust me to get your money's worth, okay?

That's a great question. And since I don't want to cut any of my services for you on either side, I can't cut my commission. You don't want any less marketing and service on your home just because you're buying one, do you? I mean after all, you can't even buy unless we get the home sold, right? So let's do the right thing and give you the full service marketing plan to get you in your next house, okay?

Wow! I would've asked that same question if I were you. And unfortunately the answer is no. I am not an agent that is willing to cut my commission. An agent who can't even stand up to you for their own worth couldn't possibly be someone you want negotiating for you when it comes time to get your price on this house, and then in turn get you the best deal on the next house, could they? That's a lot of negotiating, and doesn't it just make sense that you would want the strongest agent possible in your corner? Great, sign the contract and let's get started.

Don't cut the commission unless you want to cut the services and not guarantee the sale of your home.

That's a great question! And if these were products that I was selling, I might be able to do something. However, since I am providing a service, and actually two different services with both buying and selling a home, I can't do that. So let's get you on the way to being sold and in your new house. Just sign the contract, okay?

I know you have to ask that. And I'm sure you aren't thinking about how I'd actually be taking on twice the work and getting paid less money than if I was working with a separate buyer and seller. Look, I appreciate that you're using me for both transactions, and I'm going to show you my appreciation by getting you the best possible price on both houses. Isn't that what you really want?

～

10.   You're too new in the business.

Being new just means I am fresh and excited! Or, would you prefer one of those tired burned out agents who have been in the market for years?

So, do you want an agent that's up on all the new trends and is cutting edge? That's exactly who you'd be hiring when you hire me to do the job. Those old agents are still doing old things the old way, and this market requires an agent who has all the latest tools to do things the "new" way. Isn't that what you want?

I am new in the business. And this only means that I am going to do an even better job than those who have been doing this for years. I'm committed to getting my career started, and I know I can't start it powerfully unless I take excellent care of you, and get the job done!

Let me ask you something. Who do you think is going to have more time to focus on getting your home sold, an agent who is new in the business or, an agent who has a ton of listings where you'll just be another number? If I'm going to do whatever it takes to get your home sold, what difference does it make that I am new in the business?

Absolutely, I am new, which means that I've been trained with all the latest marketing and sales techniques. I'm sure you know that real estate has changed in just these last few years, let alone over the last decade or so. Don't you want someone who's up on the latest ideas and trends, or would you prefer someone who still bakes cookies and gives out pens to try and get your home sold?

That's valid. And let me ask you, would you rather have an agent who's new and hungry, or someone old and complacent?

∾

11.   You haven't sold any homes in our area.

I understand your concern. And while I haven't sold any homes in your specific neighborhood, I have sold 20 homes in the greater area already this year. You do want an agent that can get your home exposed to all the buyers in the marketplace, and not just your neighbors, don't you?

You're exactly right! I haven't sold any homes in your area. Since your neighborhood is only a very tiny fraction of the market, does that really matter? I mean, having sold 30 homes already this year, certainly you see the value in my marketing plan, can't you? Let's go ahead and list the home tonight, and I assure you I will get your home exposed to the entire market, and not just your neighborhood, okay?

So, do you really want to limit the sale of your home to your local area? That would cut out a lot of buyers that might come from the other areas. Wouldn't it be an advantage to have an agent who could market your property to the most possible buyers, or do you want to take a chance with an agent who only works a small geographic area?

I think you're asking because you want to be sure that the agent you list with really knows your area, is that correct? And what would happen if I could prove to you beyond a shadow of a doubt that I know the market. I know people in your neighborhood and I have previewed all the active listings. By the time I research an area, I know more about it than your mailman! Now, why don't we go over everything that's for sale in your neighborhood so we can get a clear picture of where you should be?

That's correct! And you can feel confident that my company and I have sold homes all over this area. So, we're both familiar with your neighborhood, and are working with plenty of buyers looking here. Isn't that what you want?

I understand your concern. And with homes plastered all over the internet, buyers coming in from any and everywhere, does that really matter? If you want to limit your exposure to just your neighbors, you could go with a neighborhood agent. Or, you can list with me and guarantee yourself maximum exposure. Which is better for you?

৩৯

SERVICING THE LISTING

1. We want more advertising/open houses.

I can understand that because you're just really frustrated that the house has not sold. Let me ask you, if you saw a full page color ad in USA Today everyday for a month for a great house but the price was too high, would you buy it? If I could get you a million dollars for the house I would, but that's not what the market is telling us. The market is telling us that a price reduction is in order, do you agree?

Of course you do! And what I am hearing you say is that you just want to find the fastest way to get the home sold, correct? And the faster you want the home sold the more aggressive approach we have to take. So would you want to pay for a method that has limited results, or shall we reduce the price to attract a lot of new buyers to your house?

I would totally do that if I thought it would help sell your home. Yet, it won't. Today's buyer won't come to an open house, or call on an ad if they think the property is even slightly overpriced. Rest assured, I'm doing everything I said I would do to get your home sold, as I do for all of my listings. And unfortunately, all the people who haven't looked at your home have spoken. They're saying you're overpriced. Let's reduce it by 5% and get them to make an offer, okay?

I want you to reduce your price, and I know you want more open houses. But imagine for a moment that you've hosted your fifth open house this month, lost your weekends <u>again</u>, and are wondering what's going on, all because no one wants to buy an overpriced home. Let's do the right thing, and reduce the price so we can get buyers and not lookers, okay?

That sounds great! And yet, it goes against the law of supply and demand, do you know why? There are 1000 homes on the market, so that means there's a large supply. Every month 50 homes are selling, so that's a small demand. So what will get people to demand your property, more advertising or making it the best value on the market?

Of course you want advertising and open houses. But remember when we listed the home, I showed you that less than 3% of homes sell as a direct result of an ad or an open house? I understand that you need to sell quickly, which is exactly why I feel we should reduce the price to guarantee maximum exposure. You do want more than a 3% chance of selling the home, don't you? Great! Let's reduce the price to $234,900 and get it sold, okay?

I understand. And let me ask you, if you were a buyer in today's market would you be looking through a bunch of advertisements and running around to open houses, or would you align yourself with an agent who will find you the best deal based on price, condition and location? Ok, great! So, in order to sell shouldn't we simply be the best value on the market, or reduce the price to a price that will cause it to sell?

∽

2.   We want to cancel the listing.

First of all, let me apologize that you are to this point of frustration. One thing this market it teaching us is patience. You have seen the advertising, you have all the feedback from the showings, and I want you to know that I am frustrated right along with you. Let me ask you, do you still want the house to sell? Of course you do. So, let's look at what the competition is doing and make a decision. Will you agree to that?

I want you to stick with me. And I appreciate that this has been real frustrating for you. There are 1,100 more listings on the market today than there were last year at this time. And yet, houses are still selling every day. If you are willing to be totally aggressive about what we have to do to get this house sold, then I'd be willing to meet with you tomorrow, and we'll come to a meeting of the minds about what we need to do. You do want to get the home sold, right?

Don't cancel the listing unless you want to guarantee the home not selling.

Of course you want to cancel the listing. You're frustrated with market conditions and the fact that the home hasn't sold. Let me ask you, do you still want to sell the home? Great! I'll do an updated market analysis to see exactly how we are comparing to other homes that are currently for sale, as well as those that have recently sold. Let's see if we have room to price it a bit more aggressively and get it sold, okay?

Gosh, if I were you I would probably want to cancel the listing, too. And yet, canceling the listing isn't going to get the home sold is it? I don't have to tell you, you already realize that price is critical in today's market. And in order to sell the home we really ought to consider lowering the price before the market gets even worse. Don't you agree?

I will gladly cancel your listing for you, if you allow me to shoot straight with you. Every time I've called you to report what's going on with your home, I've asked you to reduce the price, because price is the only thing that gets a home sold. And every time I've asked you, you've told me you want to stand pat. And in that time I've sold five of my other listings. So clearly, I'm getting homes sold. It's like you ignore your doctor's advice, and then get mad because you got sick. Do you really want to cancel the listing, or do you just want to get your home sold?

I understand. And do you really want to cancel the listing, or do you just want your home sold? So, we need to work together on this. I have done all of the same things that I do to sell all of my listings, yet they sell and yours hasn't. The difference? If I had to ask those other sellers for a price reduction, they reduced their price, and then they sold. You can certainly have your listing back, with no hard feelings, but all the other agents know your home is on the market. So whoever you give it to has already had ample time to bring their buyer. Unless you reduce the price, you'll get the same results. What do you want to do?

∽

3.   Why aren't you showing our house?

That's a great question. I'm not showing your house because we've had very few calls on the house. We know if the advertising we're doing and the calls we are making don't produce any interest in the house, then the house is probably overpriced. I know that's hard to hear, but look at all the places the house has been marketed, and still we have no phone calls. We need to open up a whole new market for the house by putting it in a new price range. Does that make sense?

We have shown your house every day on the internet, in print advertising and by calling people. You're absolutely right, we should be showing the house and we are. This house is being seen by every potential buyer out there, and their agent. My job is to get your home out to as many agents and their clients as possible. And you can see all the exposure we are giving you just by the number of showings. It doesn't really matter if someone else sells it, as long as you get your price, correct?

That's a great question! Remember when we listed the house we agreed that with over 1,500 agents in the market, other agents would be showing the house far more often than we would? Our job is to find the buyer no matter what agent they're working with. Ultimately, you don't really care which agent sells the home, as long as it sells, right? And in order for the buyers to choose your home versus the competition, it needs to be priced right. Don't you agree?

You know what? If we had buyers who were looking for a home like yours, and were financially qualified to buy it, we would definitely be showing it. Our job, however, is to get the home exposed to all the buyers in the market, not just the buyers I represent. Let's adjust the price down, so we can expose the home to even more buyers, okay?

Good question. And the answer is because I personally don't have a buyer looking for your specific home. As I've told you, my job as your agent is to get your home sold. Most of the time it will be my efforts, and not necessarily my buyer that gets a home sold. And as soon as I get off the phone with you I'm going back to calling all the top agents in the market, all of your neighbors in a five block radius, all of my past clients, and any buyer of mine who might be interested in a house like yours. Does that work for you?

Because I've been busy marketing your house to all of the buyer's agents in the market. The people who have been through your house are a direct result of my marketing. Isn't that what you wanted me to do, get people through your home to buy it?

༄

4.   Why aren't we getting any showings?

We listed the house in August and had seven showings that month, meaning that there was very good interest, do you agree? Then in September, we had four showings, and now in October, we've had two. Obviously you see interest is slowing down, right? You said you wanted to be moved by fall, which simply means that we need to adjust for what's happening. We could watch the showings dwindle every month, or we could get really aggressive and take some action that will boost interest. Can we discuss a plan for that?

I know. I was really surprised that we have not gotten many showings. So, I got on the computer and pulled a quick market analysis. As a matter of fact, did you know that only three houses sold in your price range in the last month? And they were all new construction. In other words, buyers are seeing more value in brand new, make sense? We need to make your home very competitive with these new houses. Do you want to meet and discuss how we can accomplish that together?

There's really only one answer to that question: the buying public thinks your house is overpriced. I wish there were other nicer reasons, and there aren't. So, would you like to reduce the price and get buyers to see your home?

Unfortunately, since we listed your house, 100 others have come on the market. So, now we need to take extraordinary measures to make your home shine in the eyes of the buyer. What do you think we should do?

I understand your concern about no showings, and I'm just as worried as you are. With over 6,000 homes on the market right now, the odds of a buyer wanting to see your home with so many to choose from are pretty low, aren't they? What do you think we can do to cause the buyers to choose your home instead of the competition?

Of course you would ask that question. I mean the home is being advertised all over the place, and being aggressively marketed by my entire team day after day, and yet it's still not being shown! It's been proven when a home isn't being shown, it's an indication that the price is too high. And in order to generate activity you need to reduce the price, shouldn't you?

ᕬ

PRICE REDUCTION OBJECTIONS

1.   We haven't been on the market long enough to lower the price.

You've been on the market for two weeks, and it's a verifiable fact that the most activity occurs when a house first comes on the market. We haven't had many showings, which actually hurts our chances to sell this house for top dollar. I am really concerned that if we don't lower the price now, we are going to lose money later. Let's get the price lowered today, okay?

I can appreciate that. And has there ever been a time when you sat back and waited for something to happen, instead of taking action? We can sit and hope things will change, or we can take some action that will cause it to change. Time and time again, we see the sooner people adjust to the market, the faster their house will sell. Let's really get aggressive and get the price down, make sense?

I can see why you would feel that way. And, do you remember when we first listed the house? I told you if we went with your price, we would need to reduce it if we weren't sold after the first thirty days. Well, we're already at 28 days. And as you know, we've had a very limited amount of activity on the home, which means the buyers aren't even choosing to look at your home. They're finding better value elsewhere. We can either continue to help the competition sell their homes, or we can get your home sold by adjusting the price. Which is better for you?

I can appreciate you feel it hasn't been for sale for long enough to reduce the price. And yet, you have to be sold and moved before October 1st, right? Since closing on a home can take a minimum of 30 days <u>after</u> you accept an offer, we're already close to missing your move date. If you want to ensure your move on time, then you should trust me, and reduce the price to $299,900. That way we can expose ourselves to a new group of buyers and get an offer. Isn't that what you want?

I agree. And do you want to be <u>proactive</u> and get it sold? Or, do you want to be <u>reactive</u> and wait for an offer that's not coming, while prices continue to drop, and your home sits on the market month after month?

I would feel the same way, unless I really wanted to get my home sold. Naturally you know that the shelf life of a new listing is between seven and 21 days. After that, no one even thinks about showing your home, unless they have a major lowball client. So, let's reduce the price now, which will cause your house to show up on the agents' daily activity sheets immediately. That will put your home in front of all the agents again, and show them you're serious about selling, okay?

❧

2. What are you doing to sell the home?

That's a natural question, thanks for asking. Would you agree the market numbers I sent show that sales have slowed down? So the question is, what can we do in a market where there are fewer and fewer buyers? You know, it's a question of supply and demand. And we have to realistically look at how we can adjust to a changing market. In order to adjust and get buyers to pay attention, all we need to do is lower the price. I know it's difficult to accept, but do you agree that we need to do that?

I'm glad you asked, after all I only get paid when I produce results for you, right? Day after day, I talk to lots of people about your house, and market it aggressively. And even doing all that, the house hasn't sold, which is frustrating for both of us. Let's set up a meeting where we can adjust quickly to this market, and get you moved. Does that make sense?

That's a great question! And I am doing exactly what I promised you I would in the written marketing plan that we both signed when we listed the home. You know, I totally get your frustration with the home not selling, and I'm on your side. I want to get the home sold as quickly as possible, too. With the current market conditions, it takes more aggressive pricing to get properties sold in a reasonable time frame. Since time is of the essence for you, it makes sense to adjust the price down to pull in buyers. Don't you agree?

What a great question! And I promise you I am doing the exact same thing for you that I have done for the other 30 homes I've sold so far this year. The challenge is that the market conditions have changed, and it is requiring more aggressive pricing to get homes sold than it has in the past. You can either just be for sale, or you can be sold. Which is better for you? Great! Let's reduce now to a price that will cause it to sell, okay?

Good question. After this call, I will fax a list of all the ads that I have run, and I'll print out the web pages from all of the sites where your home is featured. There's my personal site, my company site, realtor.com, etc. I'll also forward you a list of all the streets of all your neighbors that I've called looking for a buyer. Can you see now how I've been working for you? So, can we discuss pricing your home to sell now?

Everything I can! And I keep doing it. In fact, I've done just about everything that I did with the other 10 homes I've sold since I listed your home. You know the one difference between them and you? Those sellers reduced the price when necessary. Let's get you sold, shall we? Would a five or seven percent reduction work for you?

⟳

3.   If we reduce the price, will you reduce your commission?

That's interesting, and let me ask you a question. Has there ever been a time that you had to accept something happening that was outside your control? That time is just like this time, can I explain? The market is determining your price and it is out of our control. When your price goes down, my commission goes down. So we are both in this together, make sense? Lets work together to get this sold!

I can see where you are coming from. So let me ask you, if your boss came to you and said, "We have a big account we want you to handle and do the best job possible, but we are going to cut your pay," how do you think you'd feel about it? You hired me to do the best job possible and I am committed to doing it for you, make sense?

That's a great question! And unless you want me to reduce the marketing on the home, I can't reduce the commission. You do still want maximum exposure and marketing, don't you?

I'm sure I don't have to tell you, you already realize that you need to keep the commission competitive with other sellers in order for the agents to continue to show your home, right?

Of course I will. Reducing the price means that I get less money when the home's sold. Just sign at the bottom.

That's a great question. But let me ask why you want to penalize me for what the market is doing? Don't I still have to do my job just as well, and even work harder now than I did when it was first listed?

༄

4.   If we reduce, then we won't have any room left to negotiate.

I understand this is cutting it to rock bottom for you. And, I would rather get us priced aggressively and be in a position to turn down offers than to never get one, wouldn't you?

I clearly understand that you need to net a certain amount out of this house to get to the next one. Yet, if the house doesn't sell, you can't do anything, can you? Let's reduce to $299,900 and expect it to sell within 98 to 99 percent of the new price, okay?

I understand you don't want low offers on the house. It's a verifiable fact that when a house is priced close to market value, the offers will come in higher. So, if you'll reduce your price, then I'll put it in the multi-list as a brand new listing. Does that make sense?

I want you to sell this house for as much as possible, and I appreciate that you want to leave some wiggle room. Just imagine that we reduce the price, and the offers actually come in close to your asking price. Wouldn't that be great?

I know what you mean. And the way real estate works is, the better the perceived deal, the higher the offers that will come in. What that means is, the lower you price your house, the closer to asking you'll get. So, no negotiating will be necessary. Won't that be great?

You're right, and I'm banking that you won't <u>have</u> to negotiate. If you lower the price, then you may get multiple offers. I don't have to tell you that it may create a bidding war, which will drive up your price. You'd like that, right?

෧෨

5.   We want to wait a little longer.

Will waiting cause the market to change? Can the market get even worse as more homes sit, and home sales get even slower? You can lower the price now, or play the odds on a market that's already turning soft. Can you afford to do that?

Have you ever heard the saying, "hurry up and wait?" You want to hurry up and get the house sold, but you are telling me that you want to wait. You need to make a decision today as to whether you want the home sold, or if you are putting the brakes on. You see, my concern is that if we wait, we will be having this same conversation in 30 days, and neither of us will be happy about it. Let's speed up and get aggressive about selling the house, make sense?

Waiting longer can make the home become shopworn. Buyers won't even look at the home because it's been on the market so long. They will wonder what's wrong with it, and why it hasn't sold. You don't want to become that house, do you?

I can see why you would feel like you should wait. Yet, remember when we first listed the home? We agreed if it wasn't sold during the first 30 days, we would reduce the price to guarantee freshness and exposure to the buyers. Let's go ahead and reduce now, okay?

I understand your concern, and let me ask you a question. You've been on the market for 30 days, while rates are lower than they've been in a long time. Even so, all indicators are that prices are going to go down even further in the coming months. How will waiting benefit you in any way?

I can appreciate that, so can we go over the pros and cons of waiting? Reducing the price will cause your home to be seen again by all the agents in the market as soon as it hits the computer. It will give a fresh perspective to the agents, and will show them you're serious about selling. Buyers will be tempted to make an offer because your home will be perceived as a deal. Waiting will cause you to be lost in the thousands of listings out there, make your home a stale listing, and will have buyers avoid your home as they've been doing for the last 30 days. Which one do you want to have happen?

∽

6.   No one has even made an offer.

That's true. And when you stop and think about it, we should have had an offer by now, if the house was priced right. The National Association of Realtors says that, on the average, an offer should come in after six to seven showings. We've had ten showings and no offers. So, we should reduce the price. Does that make sense?

I know, and I am really concerned about it, just like you. Three things come into play when there are no offers. Number one is the price. The more competitive the price the faster the house will sell. Number two is condition. Homes that show like models sell faster, and for more money. And, number three is to add features. If you're not going to hire a home stager, or put in that granite counter top, then we're only talking about the price. So it sounds like we just need to get the price down, doesn't it?

Exactly! No one has even made an offer on the home because they're obviously finding better value in all the other homes that are selling. We can either be the best value on the market, or continue helping the competition sell their homes. Which is better for you?

Naturally no one has made an offer. And they aren't going to until we get the home priced at market value, and not above. I'm sure I don't have to tell you, with thousands of homes sitting on the market, the buyers are undoubtedly looking to get the best deal. Those properties are the ones that are selling. Did you want to be sold, or be priced above market value?

Exactly! This means they think it's so overpriced they won't even waste their time with an offer. So, do you want buyers to make offers, or move on?

You're right! Now, imagine you were at an auction house, and the whole audience was silent. No one was bidding on the item for sale at all. The auctioneer would either have to lower the price on the item, or risk not selling it. Which do you want to do?

༄

7.   Why don't we just offer to pay the buyer's closing costs?

You could offer to pay the buyer's closing costs. But, statistics show that if you simply reduce the price by the same amount, you will double the number of buyers interested. Wouldn't that be great?

Can I tell you why that concerns me? When buyers go on the internet to look for houses they always search by price point. So, in essence, the same buyers who haven't been making offers on your house will be the same buyers who have already seen your house, because the price is the same. Wouldn't it be more effective to just lower the price to attract a whole new group of buyers to your house? Don't you think we should take the action that will have the most impact?

We could do that, and no one will really know. You know, when someone wants to see a house they typically only look at the location they want to be in, the number of bedrooms and features of the house, and the price of the house. So, if someone wants three bedrooms and wants to live in your neighborhood, they'll possibly look at your home, if it's in their price range. Closing costs aren't even in their mind at that point. Clearly we need to do something that gets them at the search point. Your house is where it is, and you're not adding a fourth bedroom. So, the only thing you can do is reduce the price, shouldn't you?

That sounds valid, and actually that's like offering someone mustard but no hotdog. Buyers only look at price when deciding if they want to actually go through your home. If you want to pay for their closing costs, that's something we tell the agent of the buyer who has already decided they want to see your house. The way to get them to see the house is to reduce the price. So do you want to reduce it five or seven percent?

Instinctively it does make sense to do that. And it seems like you somehow feel as though you will be netting more money by paying the buyers closing costs, instead of just lowering the price. And actually it is the same to you, as the seller, either way. I recommend we simply reduce the price by the amount that you are willing to pay toward closing costs and get the house exposed to a new group of buyers, okay?

I can see where you would consider paying closing costs. And let me ask you, if you were a buyer looking for a home, would you be looking for the best priced house or the one offering to pay closing costs? Shouldn't we simply lower the price?

∽

8.   No feedback has said our price was too high.

So we can wait, and we can have this discussion again in two weeks. Or, we can reduce the price now to get some offers. You see, whether they are saying it or not, it's always about the price. Buyers compare homes with similar features and benefits and put offers in on the best deals. Lets make your house one of <u>those</u>, okay?

So let me ask you, if it's not the price, what is it? Let's pretend that you are out shopping for a car. Do you select one based on the features and benefits for the price? Of course you do, every time! Don't you think that when people are looking for a house, they are also looking for the most features and benefits for the price? And since you agree, we need to look at increasing the features, <u>or</u> reducing the price. Which would be best for you?

Of course you think that. You're concentrating on the people who went through your house, while I'm concentrating on the market. In the time we've been on the market, three of your competing homes have sold, and you haven't received an offer. That feedback tells me your home is so overpriced that you're actually helping to sell your competition. Is that what you're looking to do?

Actually no feedback <u>is</u> feedback. So far, you're the only person in the whole entire market who thinks you're home is worth $300,000. So, do you want to fight against the current, or go with the flow and get your home sold?

That's true it hasn't, but the buyers lack of interest has. Otherwise, don't you think they would've made an offer by now?

Naturally the feedback hasn't said the price is too high. There are tons of homes sitting on the market, not selling, at prices that are too high. So, buyers and agents have gotten used to this. The problem is the buyers are choosing the properties that are priced at or below market value. And, if we want to be sold, shouldn't we join that group? Or, did you want to continue just having showings, and no offers?

࿘

9.   We're going to take it off the market, and wait for the market to get better.

You could do that, and it'll really delay you building the new home, won't it? And what would happen if you missed a buyer because you were trying to predict the future? You see, we really don't know when the market will get better or worse, do we? So stick with me, and I will keep you informed of what is selling in your price range, and what we need to do to get it sold. Does that work for you?

Yes, you can take it off the market, but that won't get the home sold. And you told me when we started this process that you wanted to be moved by winter, didn't you? It's perfectly normal to be frustrated and disappointed when you expected everyone who came to see the house to buy it. The fact is the market's slower now. So, it requires real patience to hang in there. And all there is to do is adjust to what's happening. If you leave the house on the market, then I'll set up a time that we can look at the whole picture, okay?

Don't take it off the market unless you want to risk losing even more money. What if the market gets worse instead of better?

Naturally you want to take it off the market and wait for things to get better. Yet after paying the mortgage on the house month after month, hoping the market gets better, what if it doesn't, and you've lost even more? Doesn't it just make sense to go ahead and price the home for today's market, get it sold, and move into your new home while interest rates are still so favorable?

That's an option, if you plan on keeping your home for the next five to ten years. Is that what you want?

That makes sense. So are you saying that you just want to keep the home for the foreseeable future? Then taking it off the market is the worst thing you can do, can I explain? If you wait for the market to get better, interest rates may go up as well. So, while your house may be worth more, less and less people will be able to afford it. And what's worse, when you go to buy your next home, it'll cost you much more as well. Don't you just want to get it sold now and move on?

૭૦

"**N**OW What Do I Say?"

WORKING WITH BUYERS –
SIGN/AD CALLS, FLOOR DUTY, OPEN HOUSES, SHOWINGS

1.   We just want to drive by/Just give me the address.

Of course, and so if you drive by, when would that be? I want you to drive by, and be really comfortable that it's a neighborhood you want and a house that appeals to you. And can I tell you a little secret? Nine times out of ten the house looks better on the inside then it does on the outside. It just makes sense to see the inside while you're there, doesn't it?

Are you the type that judges a book by its cover? Can I tell you what is so exceptional about this property? It has an incredibly landscaped back yard that is so perfect. Do you have kids or animals? Good, because you are going to love this house. And since you can't see the yard from the road, would it make sense to actually view the property with me?

I encourage you to drive by, and I'll do you one better. Why don't you come to my office, and I'll make a list of all the available houses in that area that meet your needs. You can take your time and compare prices and features. Then, if you still want to drive by, you'll have all the addresses, or we can go through the houses you like the most. What price range do you want me to look for?

Okay, so it sounds like you're just starting to look at homes, is that right? Would it be a benefit to you if I rounded up all the houses that fit your criteria, so you could drive by all of them? I can call you back in about ten minutes, or you can stop by my office and pick them up. Which is better for you?

I understand that you just want to ride by. And since you'll already be out there, why don't I meet you and go ahead and let you see the inside of the house? It's much larger and has much more to offer than it appears from the outside. I promise there will be no pressure whatsoever. If the house doesn't work for you, I can get you access to everything that is currently for sale, based on what you are looking for. That way we can ensure you have access to all the options. What time this afternoon would work for you?

Since the outside of the home doesn't really do it much justice, why don't I meet you over there and let you see the inside? Would today at two or three work for you?

༄

2. **We just started looking.**

So, you are just looking? Don't look unless you are ready to buy a house. Can I explain? Sooner or later, you're going to see something you really want. And you'll need an agent, like me, to help you with the pre-approval and standard negotiations so that you don't buy a money pit. Working with me means that you'll have help every step of the way to make the right decision. Isn't that what you want?

Looking is good! It's the first step to discovering what you really want in a house. Would it make sense to take the next step and look together at everything on the market that matches your wish list?

Great! And since it normally takes about three to six months from when you start to look to when you close on the house you buy, when do you plan on being in your new home?

Oh, good for you! So, have you noticed how overwhelming it can be with all the ads and websites and signs out there? If you'd like, I can help weed everything out for you. Simply tell me what you're looking for in a home, what price range you want to be in, and where you want to look, and I'll have only those homes automatically emailed to you everyday. Will that work for you?

I understand. And would you like me to set you up with a local lender to get pre-qualified, and be better prepared when you find the home you want?

Perfect! And tell me what are you looking for in a home? I may have some other listings that will suit your needs. And if not, how about I get you access to all of the homes that are currently for sale? This way you'll be sure not to miss out on something, okay?

I understand you are just getting started, which is exactly why we need to get together. I can make sure that you have access to everything that is out there, and to explain the entire process to you so you'll know exactly what you're doing. My services to you are completely free and at no obligation. Can we get together today or tomorrow?

∾

3.   We're already working with an agent.

Ok, great! So has your agent gotten you access to all of the homes that are currently for sale based on what you are looking for? And are they keeping you posted daily as anything new comes available? I would be happy to do this for you today. Let me ask you a few questions so that I can be clear on what you are looking for. Do you have a few moments? Before we go forward, you didn't sign a contract with that agent did you?

Are you actually working with an agent, or have they just shown you a few homes? I don't want to step on toes or anything like that. I just want to make sure that you are getting the very best service that you can from a buyer's agent. Do you have a few minutes for me to tell you all the ways that we can help you, at no expense to you?

Don't switch agents unless you literally want to find out about new listings before they hit the internet. As one of the top listing agents in the area, I already know of properties before they even hit the market. How would it be, if you could get a head start on all the other buyers you're competing with?

So, is your agent on vacation, or too busy working with other buyers to take care of you today?

I completely understand. And so how come you're agent isn't calling me? I mean clearly you found this property before your agent did. So how come you're doing all the work? You called on an ad for a home that's been on the market for over 2 weeks. Do you think you would benefit from getting all of the listings that fit your needs as soon as they come on the market? Perfect! So, let's get together, and we'll see if this house you called on works for you. And in case it doesn't, we'll set you up so that you get every house that fits your needs as soon as they come on the market, sound good?

I understand. So are you saying if I show you this house and you like it, then you'll go back to the other agent to make an offer?

෴

4. I'm sitting in front of the house. Can you show it to me now?

I would love to show it to you now, and that house needs an appointment to be shown. I can call the seller and schedule an appointment. Just give me a number to reach you, and I'll call you right back. Are you available later today, or tomorrow?

I would love to. And unfortunately, I can't even get in the door unless I have a buyer's full name, address, phone number, email and they're pre-qualified. Have you spoken to a lender?

I could come over right now, however we need to let the sellers know we are coming and give them a bit of notice. Is there any way we could set an appointment to meet there tomorrow at noon? Ok, great! Let me set that up with the seller, and I'll call you back to confirm and give you all the information about the home. Can I ask you a few quick questions now to make sure I take excellent care of all of your needs?

Yes we can definitely take a look at this home, and the price is $299,900. Can you meet me at my office, so we can make an appointment with the sellers and give them a few minutes to clear out of the house? And when you get here, I can quickly go over all the details of this home, and the entire home buying process so you'll be sure to understand all your options, okay?

Well, I could show it to you now, but the sellers require an appointment. What I can do right now is meet with you, so we can discuss what you are looking for and what the payment would be on this house. Could you meet with me in about 20 minutes?

Great! And I would like to be your agent. The house is vacant so it's very easy to show, but I am not in the general area at the moment. Will you meet with me at 2:00PM today and I will have my lender call you in the meantime and go over everything. And if it is the house you want, you will be prepared to make an offer, okay?

∽

5.   We want look at houses first, and then we'll get pre-qualified.

Ouch. Can I tell you why that might be the worst thing you could do? Getting pre-qualified costs you nothing. It obligates you to nothing. And, yet it saves you so much aggravation in the end. Can I explain? Let's say you find the home you love, but unfortunately, you don't qualify for that price range. Or, you find out the monthly payment is higher than you want to pay. Then you've just wasted your own valuable time, and gotten your hopes up for nothing. That's not what you want, is it? I have a lender than can get you pre-qualified over the phone in minutes. Let's make a quick call, okay?

That seems to make sense. And just suppose you find the house you want, but the seller won't accept your offer without pre-qualification. You risk losing the home because you're trying to put the cart before the horse. If you were selling your house, would you want to deal with someone whose qualifications you didn't know?

I can understand that you would prefer to start with the fun part first. Yet, my concern is that we may end up finding the perfect house for you, and then discover it is much higher in price than you're comfortable paying. You don't want to get your heart set on something and then not be comfortable spending that amount of money, do you?

Don't look at homes first unless you want to have an overwhelming, frustrating experience finding the right home. I mean, if we're going to get you the best deal on the home, don't you think the sellers would be more willing to negotiate with you, especially if you come prepared with your loan approval letter in hand? Additionally, don't you want to look at homes priced in a range that will give you the type of monthly payment that you want, as opposed to taking a shot in the dark?

I'm concerned about that, can I explain? This is what happened to a couple I was working with: they wanted to look at houses and found one they absolutely loved! Then they went to get pre-qualified, and found out that someone else's bad credit was on their credit report by mistake. By the time we straightened it out, the house had sold. They were just devastated. It was like calling off a wedding and sending everybody home. That's not what you want, is it?

Let me ask you, have you read about how banks are tightening up on lending? And how the rate could change depending on your credit score? Doesn't it make sense to find out what interest rate you will get, so we know what your payments will be?

☙

6.   We want to look at properties with the listing agents.

Okay, so what you're saying is that you want no one to represent your best interests in the transaction. You do know that listing agents work primarily for their sellers, right?

I understand, and can I ask why you want to shoot yourself in the foot? The listing agent is going to do everything they can to get you to buy <u>that</u> house. A buyer's agent working for you will want you to choose the house that's best suited for you. They have no vested interest in <u>what</u> house you buy. They only have your best interest at heart. Isn't that what you want?

Naturally you want to look with the listing agent. That's because you feel you'll get a better deal, or something, don't you? And what you're actually doing is allowing yourself to be unprotected, while the listing agent is representing the seller, and looking out for their best interests. Honestly, you'll get the best deal by having a powerful agent, like me, representing and negotiating on your behalf. You don't want to have the seller's agent working against you, do you?

I understand that you would want to look with the listing agent, and can I tell you want concerns me about that? There is no one there to look out for you. The listing agent looks out for the seller. And you are left to negotiate for yourself, and hopefully find your way through all the legalities, paperwork, inspections, loan process and finally, all the details for the closing. Wouldn't it just make sense to have your own agent to do all that for you?

Let me ask you, would you use an attorney that represents the opposing side? Of course not, because that would work against you. Yet, that's exactly what you are doing by looking at properties with listing agents. Listing agents work directly against you getting the house at a good price. Did you know that?

What specifically causes you to believe that you'll get good service from an agent who's not representing you? The listing agent has a legally binding agreement with the seller to try to get them top dollar. They really don't care that you want a good deal. What listing agent will walk that fine line of trying to represent both sides fairly?

What I sense is, you think the listing agent will save you money. Can I tell you how that will actually work against you? You're not saving one dime by going directly to the listing agent. The seller has already agreed to pay six percent commission, whether it gets split with a buyer agent, or not. You're literally paying the listing agent six percent to negotiate the highest possible price on the seller's behalf. Is that what you want?

❧

7.   How much will the seller come down?

I wish I knew. The best way to find out is to make an offer. When do you want to close?

In my opinion, based on how long they've been on the market, I'd say they probably will negotiate. But what I think, and what someone will do once there's a legitimate offer on the table are two completely different things. Let's make an offer and see how negotiable they are, okay?

You know, that's something we haven't even discussed yet. We just listed the property last week and we've had a ton of showings so far, with lots of interest. The best thing to do is, meet me at the property to see if it's something that will even work for you. And, if you like it, we can make whatever offer you feel comfortable with, and see if the seller will accept it, okay?

Naturally you would ask that because you want to make sure you are getting the best deal possible in this market, don't you? Why don't we meet over there and I'll bring the market analysis, which will show you what the current market is bearing for the property. And if you like the home, you can make an offer based on that research, and your gut feeling. Then we can see what the seller will agree to. Would today or tomorrow work best for you?

Well, it really doesn't matter what they do. What matters is that you write an offer that works for you, right?

Suppose they don't come down and they're just firm on their price. After all, they've already dropped the price by $20,000. What would you do in their shoes if you had dropped your price to rock bottom? Just imagine that you buy the house at this wholesale price, instead of full retail like you would have six months ago. Let's work this soft market and get you the house.

∽

8.   We want to look at more homes before we make an offer.

That makes a lot of sense. And so I can better help you, what do you need to find in another house to make this one go away?

Okay, we can do that. And since when we met, I showed you how these five homes were the best available based on what you want and need, what specifically are you looking to find in homes that fit <u>less</u> of your criteria?

Don't look at other homes unless you're prepared to lose this home. We're the fourth showing this week so far.

Looking at more homes might mean you're just scared to make a mistake, right? And if we looked at the market and you felt like you were paying a fair price, and we made the contract contingent on a home inspection, you'd start to feel comfortable, right?

Great! How does this sound? Let's look at two more homes first thing in the morning. That way you'll be <u>absolutely</u> sure that this is the right house. And if we look at two more homes and they're not as nice as this one, you'll be ready to write a contract on this one, correct?

I can appreciate that you would want to look at other homes. And has there ever been a time when you knew something was perfect for you, and you waited to make a move on it, and in the end lost out on it? Well this time could be just like that time, may I explain? If you don't make an offer on this house today, it could very well be sold by the time you come back to it. Since it meets all of your needs, is priced well, and is in the school district that you desire, shouldn't you buy this home?

You could do that. And yet, the more homes you look at, the more confused you may become. Since this house has exactly what you're looking for, and is priced well, why don't we go ahead and make an offer on this one?

∽

9.   We want to make a low ball offer, and see what happens.

Of course you want to come in low, and yet you really want to get this house, don't you? May I tell you why coming in so low concerns me? See, if we come in that low we may actually offend the seller, and cause them to be less negotiable than if we came in with a reasonable offer. And in the end, this could cause you to pay even more for the house than if we started out a bit more in the ballpark, does that make sense? Great! Let's offer ten percent less than list price and see if we can get this house for you, okay?

I can see where you're coming from, and yet this house has only been on the market 23 days. It's in immaculate condition and has already been shown eight times, with other buyers thinking of writing offers. If you want to ensure that you get this house, and don't lose it to one of those other buyers, then you should trust me and offer within 95% of the list price, okay?

I understand completely, and you can try that. But don't lowball unless you're ready to lose this house, can I explain? You can lowball and have the sellers so upset that they won't even sell you the house. I've seen it happen over and over. They get offended and, nine times out of ten, they won't even make a counteroffer. So, instead of losing the house, let's make an offer that is almost what we think they'll bite at. And maybe they'll take it, make sense?

It's just natural to want to get the house for the best price. Help me understand how I'll explain to the sellers all the reasons behind your offer, because they may feel you might be trying to steal their house, right? So, can you give me all the reasons why they should take a lowball offer, so it makes sense to them? Because without good reasons, they may just throw your offer out, and that's not what you want, is it?

Ok, that makes sense. So, are you saying that you don't really want the house, or were you just trying to get a fair deal? Then clearly you need to come in at a reasonable and fair price, so that you can actually get this house, or you can lose this house and always wish you would have bought it. Which is better for you?

I understand. And it sounds to me like you just want to make sure you're getting a good deal, correct? Why don't we pretend we're the sellers and do a comparative market analysis on this house, to see if they're priced right? If they are, then you'll need to decide how badly you want the house, and make a fair offer. If they're not, then let's come in where the market analysis says they should be, okay?

You could do that. And how do you think you'd feel if someone came along and put in a lowball offer on your home? Your initial reaction is how this seller will feel. Do you want to start off your negotiations like that, or do you actually want to get the home?

᭜

NEGOTIATING OFFERS – SELLERS

1. I want full price.

We can wait for a full price offer, but what if it never comes? In a perfect world, everyone would get full price or more, but you've seen we're not in that perfect market. If I could wave a magic wand and make it happen for you, I would. But the truth is we need to wrap our arms around any offer that comes along in this market and hug it. Don't you agree?

Let me ask you, have you ever been shopping in a store where everything is full price? Don't you automatically look for the "sale signs" and go there first? Well, the same thing happens when people are shopping for a house! They want to feel like they got a little bit of a sale, and a little money off. So, if you were looking for a house, would you look for the ones that were "full price only," or would you look for sellers who might be flexible to start negotiations?

I do, too! And if this wasn't the only offer in 45 days, I'd say we have a leg to stand on. And if you want to move, you'll naturally want to take this offer so that you <u>can</u> move, don't you think?

I understand, and unfortunately this buyer is only willing to pay $345,000. If you can move in the time that you want, and be done with all of the hassle of selling your home, is it really worth it to try and haggle over five grand, and maybe upset the buyer to the point of backing out?

You want full price? I'm curious as to why you feel you'll ever get full price? Remember when we listed the home and we looked at the market analysis together? It showed the average list to sale price ratio was 96%, and I showed you how mine is 99%. Well, this offer is 98% of your asking price. So, shouldn't we at least counter back at 99% and see if we can get it sold for you?

Don't expect full price unless you want the house to sit on the market for a long, long time. There's way too much for the buyers to choose from, for them to consider offering <u>any</u> seller full price right now.

༄

2.   I'm not paying closing costs.

Don't pay closing costs unless you want to get the house sold. You see, most of the buyers in this market haven't saved enough money to make the down payment and pay their own closing costs. It shouldn't be that way, but the facts are about half the buyers can't afford your house right now. And if you want to sell this home, you'll need to help with closing costs.

Being willing to pay closing costs might actually save you money, can I explain? You need to be in the new house in 90 days, have this house sold, and that's the perfect outcome for your family. Houses are on the market right now an average of 100 days, and some houses are taking longer. Are you concerned about making double payments? Paying closing costs for a buyer now might save you money in the long run, because you won't <u>have</u> to make double payments. Does that make sense?

Ok, so what I'm hearing you say is you want to have your cake and eat it too, is that correct? In negotiations, both parties need to feel like they got something in the deal. So, you have your price, you have your settlement date and all they want is help with the closing costs. Doesn't it make sense to do that?

I can appreciate that, and let's think about it as an insurance policy. You're going to get $4,000 less for your home than you wanted in order to insure that you sell it, and get to Tulsa by February. Isn't that worth it?

I can understand that you feel like you shouldn't have to pay the buyers closing costs. I don't want you to have to pay it either. And yet, when we figure the bottom line here with the closing costs included, you are still netting exactly what you were looking to walk away with. So, does it really matter that we pay the closing costs, if it means we get the home sold and you profit the amount you wanted?

Of course you don't want to pay the buyers closing costs, because you feel that should be their responsibility, don't you? And yet, if it means selling the house, shouldn't we simply agree and move forward?

☙

3.   I'm not going to give it away.

You know I can appreciate your saying that, and I don't want you to give it away. In fact, if you do, I'm taking it! What it sounds like you're saying, is you that you just want to make the most money possible, right? The house has been on the market for 45 days, and only has three showings. In this current market, I want you to trust me and accept this offer. Remember, the longer the home is on the market, the less you end up with.

I totally get where you are coming from, and with what's going on in the market, you're definitely not giving it away. In fact, you should feel blessed that we've gotten this offer, after the length of time the home has been sitting. Let's sign the contract now before prices go down even more, okay?

That's perfect, because I don't want you to give it away either. So, before we get upset at the number, let's appreciate the fact that we got an offer. Now, what would be a nice counter offer that says, "I'm selling, but I'm not giving it away"?

That's a valid concern. And so far, you're the highest bidder for your home. So, unless you want to outbid the competition, and buy your home back, I'm going to suggest we take this offer. Or, we can sit here for 90 more days and hope someone else comes along. Which is better for you?

Of course. Help me understand when you say "give it away." What is the bottom line number that you won't go below? Ok, great! Now let's talk about a range in between that bottom line number and your asking price. And if you could put a check in your pocket right now for say 10%

over your bottom line, would you take it? Well, guess what? When you do the math, this offer is actually <u>12%</u> over your bottom line. So, let's take the money and run, okay?

No, you don't need to give it away. The best offers that come together are where the seller feels like they got what they deserve out of the house. Maybe not what they dream they will get, but a number that works to get them to the next house. And buyers feel good if they can tell everyone they negotiated something off the price. So, we're going to work together to find that place where both you and the buyer feel good. How does that sound?

∾

4.   I want to wait for a better offer.

I can understand that you would want to wait for a better offer. And what I hear you saying is that you want to ensure the most money, right? The first offer is generally the best offer, and the longer a house sits on the market the harder it is to sell. So, surely you can see how accepting this offer is the best way to net the most money, can't you?

That makes sense that you think we should wait for a better offer to come along. And may I tell you what concerns me about that? What if we turn down this offer, and don't get another for months? Every month you're losing thousands of dollars, while hoping for another offer that may never come, or might be less than this one. In the end, do you really think this is your best option? Or, should we simply accept this offer now, and guarantee you the most money?

No problem, how long do you want to wait? Would you wait six months to a year? Because that's how long it might take before we see this market get better. And I think we have to consider that it may not get better for a long time. I'm afraid if you wait the offers will actually come in worse, not better. Can you afford to take that chance?

Can I tell you what just happened to some people who decided to wait for a better offer last month? They had an offer the first week their house was on the market and they decided to wait for a better offer. Well, they sincerely regret it now, because they realize there is no better market when the market is going down. They should have embraced the first offer and taken it without even thinking. And if they had, they'd be happy in their new home by now. How about we take another look at this offer, and see if we can work with it, okay?

I understand. And have you heard the saying that a bird in the hand is worth two in the bush? You have this offer in hand, and yet there're no offers in the bush. So you're gambling that some unforeseen person will swoop down and make a better offer with better terms and a better closing date. What are those odds?

You can do that, but I'm going to have to give you back your listing. In my professional opinion, this is an offer you should consider by making a counter, or accepting as is. If you think there's a better offer waiting for you, I don't know where it's coming from, and I guess I really can't help you. Maybe there's a super agent out there who can circumvent the market, and you'd be better off with him or her. Why don't we work together on this offer and get your house sold?

∽

NEGOTIATING OFFERS - BUYERS

1.   What if I pay too much for the house?

You know, that's a great question! And did you know that real estate has gone up every decade for the last 160 years? Sure, there will be down markets. And ultimately, it will be worth more in the long run, just like the house you grew up in, right? Frankly, you can feel safe that you're going to pay a fair price. Does that work for you?

That's definitely a valid concern. And the more you think about it, the more you already realize that even <u>thinking</u> of making an offer means the house is priced well enough for your consideration. What closing date do you want to put on the contract?

I totally understand, and so the question is what is too much? Let's go over the active and sold listings and look at the value of the house in today's market. If you are willing to do that, then I'm willing to help the seller understand what we've come up with, make sense?

When you stop and think about it, that's a natural fear around any house you might see. Everyone wants to make sure they got the best deal for the money. You can trust me, that almost every buyer has a fear of paying too much. And that's exactly why you have me to advise you, right?

Naturally you would bring that up. And that's exactly why I'm here to do all the homework with you, and structure an offer that gets you a good solid deal on the house. Let's meet tonight and go over everything, okay?

I'm going to make sure you don't pay too much for the house. And if we can't negotiate a great deal for you with the seller, then we simply find another home for you and move forward. Know that I am only here to look out for your best interests and protect you every step of the way. Trust me, okay?

❦

2.   What would you do if you were me?

I appreciate that. And what I think you're saying is you just want to make sure you're making the right decision, correct? So, if you knew you were going to have an appraisal and a team of inspectors representing you, would that take some of your concern away? Good! Let me explain the clauses we'll put in the contract for your protection, okay?

Great question! And just so you know I do this <u>all</u> the time, and every situation is different. On a scale of one to ten, with 1 being the lowest and 10 being the highest, how comfortable are you? And what would make you feel more comfortable that you were making the right choice?

Good question. Personally, I would do the deal at that price. But don't misunderstand me, I'm not telling you to do that. I'm comfortable knowing that even if I paid a little too much today, real estate always goes up over the long haul. But, that's just me. What do you think?

I don't want to tell you what to do with your money. I sell real estate. I don't give financial advice. What I would do, is tell you if I thought the price is too high for the market. And, in my opinion it isn't. Does that work for you?

Thanks for trusting my opinion. What I recommend is meet in my office, and I'll do a market analysis for you. Then you can see exactly what the market value of the home should be on paper. That way, we can structure an offer that you feel comfortable with, and see if we can get this house for you. After all, it is exactly what you've been looking for, and you do really want it, don't you?

I would be willing to pay pretty close to full price on this house. It's only been on the market for two weeks, it's immaculate, and it's already priced well for today's market. After looking at all those other houses, I'm sure you already realize this home is just right for you, isn't it? Great! Let's write up an offer, okay?

∽

3.   I know what the seller paid ___ years ago.

Yes they did pay that. And what we need to do, is find out exactly what they've done to the home since they bought it. Also I'll run a market analysis to see what the home is worth today. Then we will structure the offer from there. I mean, if we can get the home at fair market value you do want to buy it, don't you?

That's a valid concern, and yet you do want this home, don't you? Then all we need to do is simply make the best offer you feel you are willing to pay, while not coming in too low where we'll offend the seller into being less negotiable. So, what price would you be willing to pay for this home?

That's the great thing about public records; you can get some very useful information. And when you stop and think about it, the market has gone up five percent a year since the sellers bought the house. Plus they added a new kitchen and put in hardwood floors. So, when we add that all up, it works out to their asking price, which just validates we're in the same ballpark. Isn't that great?

That's an interesting point. And what I think you really want is to just make sure you pay a fair price for this, am I correct? And since the seller bought the house ten years ago, and we don't know what shape it was in at that time, it may not impact what the value is today. Let's look at the comparative market analysis I did and see if it's in line, so you do pay a fair price, all right?

Yeah, the tax records said they paid $250,000. Unfortunately, what they paid has no bearing on the price today. The only people who determine the price of the house are the buying public. The question is do you want this house? If not, we can keep looking and try to find a similar house, probably priced the same, with maybe a less negotiable seller, or we can key in on the house you liked enough to already make an offer, and buy it. Which do you prefer?

I can appreciate that, and are you saying if you found the exact same house right next door but knew that those owners paid more for their house when they bought it, it'd be okay with you? All you need to do is determine if you want this house or not. So, what do you say?

∽

4.   They're asking too much.

They're asking too much? I'm curious, what specifically causes you to believe they're asking too much? The market analysis shows they are priced exactly where they should be, which means you can buy this home even at full list price and feel comfortable knowing that you got a nice deal. And hopefully, we'll be able to negotiate an even better price. Let's crunch the numbers and make an offer, okay?

Imagine for a moment that we go ahead and make the best offer we can, and they meet us somewhere in the middle, and you get the home of your dreams at a price that you can feel at peace with.

They may be asking too much. And the longer it stays on the market the more negotiable they should be. So why don't we call the agent and ask if they are getting flexible?

What I really think you are concerned about is overpaying for the house, is that right? The house just came on the market, you've seen all the cards on the counter and we know there might be other interest. The agent said there are two showings tomorrow morning, so we need to be realistic about what might happen. Do you feel in your heart that this is the right house? Good, then do the right thing for yourselves and lets get it for you, okay?

Could be, and unless you make an offer you'll never know. What price do you want to start at?

I understand your concern. Yet if you look at all the comparatives in the area, you'll find they're within range. Let's make an offer and see what happens, okay?

ᡣ

5.   It needs too much work.

You're right. It does need a lot of work, which leaves a lot of room for profit, too. What if we could get the house at an excellent price, leaving you plenty of room to make the repairs and improvements, and have instant equity? Would that work for you?

I agree. It does need too much work. Let's go find another house that's in better condition. Or, we can make an offer at a number you'd be comfortable paying, in light of the work that you will need to do. Which is better for you?

It does need work. So, let's get a good contractor in to see if it makes sense to fix it up exactly the way you want it. Just imagine that you got the home for a price that would allow you to upgrade it. That would pretty exciting, wouldn't it?

You're right. It does need a lot of work. But, can you imagine what this house could be once you get it fixed up? Can you see yourself in the dining room with your entire family at Thanksgiving? And you wanted to have the same kitchen as your old house, so here's your chance! It could actually work out perfectly for you in the long run. Don't you agree?

I agree. Yet, lots of that work will be taken care of in the home inspection. The seller will either repair the items, or give you a credit at closing. Which would be better for you?

Of course it does. The neighborhood average is $500,000 and you only want to look up to four hundred. Do you want to change neighborhoods, or price ranges?

〇〜〇

6.   I won't go any higher than this.

Of course you won't go any higher, unless you want the house. And, if you do go higher, your payment will only go up fourteen dollars a month. That's not much, is it?

Sometimes the reason buyers will not go higher on a house is because they are not sure it's really the house for them. Are you feeling that way? Because you could lose the house, and as long as you're not attached to the outcome, we can certainly start over. Although, I hope interest rates don't go up which would cost you much more in the long run. Do you agree?

Don't stand firm unless you want to lose this house.

That makes sense, if you feel like looking at more houses over the next few months. Is that what you want?

I understand that you don't want to pay more than this for the home. And, what it sounds like is you're worried about paying too much for the house, am I right? Well, based on the market analysis, do you realize you are actually paying less than what the market is currently bearing for the home?

I can appreciate that you don't want to go any higher than this. And, I don't want you to pay more for the house than you are comfortable. Since this is the tenth home we've looked at, which one of the other nine would you want to buy if this doesn't work out? Or, do you want to go ahead and pay the extra few thousand to have the best house of what's available?

෴

"**Now** What Do I Say?"

NEGOTIATING HOME INSPECTIONS – SELLERS

1.   These repairs are going to cost thousands.

It does seem that way right now. And what we need to do is get a written estimate from a licensed contractor to give us an exact quote. Then we can make an educated decision on how to respond to the buyers, okay? Do you have a licensed contractor in mind? If not, I can refer you to ours and have him come out tomorrow.

I want you to make the repairs, and I can totally appreciate that it is a lot of unexpected money. And yet, if we don't agree to the repairs, the buyer can choose to walk away. Then we are legally obligated to either fix <u>all</u> the repairs, or disclose them to the next buyer. And who knows how long it may take to find that next buyer. You don't want to go through all that, do you?

It's quite possible, and you know what the good thing is? You won't have to spend any money out of pocket. You'll have the option of repairing or replacing the items, or giving a credit at closing that simply comes out of your proceeds. Which one works for you?

Yes, you have to fix these items. But, you'd have to do that for any other buyer. And if you're committed to moving, then you'll definitely need to do the repairs. Or, did you want the buyer to walk?

They could cost thousands, but that's not typically what we see for these kinds of repairs. And you can trust me that most home inspectors put their estimates on the high side, so they don't get blamed later. Doesn't it make sense to get the facts first?

Gee, I hope not, for your sake! Let's divide these repairs into two groups, major and minor. Let's look at the two lists and price out the major repairs first, and see what number we use for that. Then we'll look at the minor repair list, and start weeding those out. If you'd be willing to fix the major items, then I'd be willing to bet that the buyers will forget about a lot of the minor items. Sound fair?

🙼

2.   I'm selling the house "as/is."

Of course you're selling the house "as/is." Yet, the buyer asked you to fix a safety issue, which you didn't even know about. So, this is a huge surprise, isn't it? I appreciate where you're coming from, and what would happen if you just gave the buyer a $500 credit to accept the problem so you could get moved?

You can sell the house "as/is," but that would normally mean a discounted price, okay?

Sure, I understand. However, you do know that legally we have to disclose this information, which is probably going to mean a price reduction if we put it back on the market. Should we do that, or agree to fix these items?

Ok, you can do that. But first we have to lose this buyer, and second we need to reduce the price on your listing by about ten thousand dollars to balance out the fact that you won't be taking care of anything. Should I get the price reduction in the multi-list, or break the bad news to the buyer's agent first?

Of course we are selling the home "as/is," which means that we aren't obligated to do any of this. However, the buyers have the option to walk away. Did you want to get the deal closed, or take the chance of it all falling apart here at the end?

We are selling the home "as/is." And, I bet you feel a bit taken advantage of at this point after coming down off the price, agreeing to pay their closing costs and now being asked to make repairs, don't you? Many sellers feel just like you do, and unfortunately this would be the same with any buyer. Even you, as a buyer, would probably feel the same about these repairs, wanting the home to be safe before you move your family in, wouldn't you? Let's go ahead and get the repairs done, so you can put all this behind you and move forward. Isn't that what you really want?

༺༻

3.   I'm not paying someone to do this, I can do it myself.

Don't use a licensed contractor unless you want to be totally free and clear of this house once we close. If you choose to do it yourself, and something goes wrong, the buyers can then come back to you after closing. You don't really want to deal with that possibility, do you?

I don't want you to pay a licensed contractor either. I realize that doing it yourself could save you some money. Yet, I want you to do what is necessary to get the deal closed, and not have the buyers walk away. You don't want to take that chance, do you?

Oh my! I had a seller who decided to do the work themselves on another transaction and the buyer didn't like it. The seller had to then hire someone to actually verify the work was up to code. And they had to pay the inspector, so it actually cost him more to do the work. And what happens if there's an electrical problem, and the buyer blames you? The best way to protect yourself from liability is to hire a professional, don't you agree?

You are totally capable of doing the work yourself, but the buyers don't know that. If you do the work yourself, how can we make them feel comfortable that you have the expertise to do it yourself? Would you be willing to pay a home inspector to verify what you have done?

You know what, that's a good idea. Except for the fact that you will forever be on the hook should those items fail. Do you want to be sitting around in your new house six months from now and get a bill for the repairs of a garbage disposal because this guy claims you messed it up?

I understand, and yet the buyer is insisting that it's done by a professional. Do you want the buyer to back out over a few hundred dollars in repairs? If you were the buyer, would you trust the seller to do the work, instead of a professional?

❧

4.   The buyer's just being picky.

Don't you just love it? I see it every day. And the reason some buyers are so picky is that they are just plain scared. They are scared that there is something they might miss, or scared that they will make a mistake. Were you scared when you bought your first house? I was too. And let's remember this <u>really is</u> their first house. So, what could we do to make them more comfortable about it?

I know. Yet, I've seen situations like this work out time and time again. They may just want to be heard, and get a little complaining out of their system. It doesn't mean they won't take the house. Let's give them twenty-four hours to calm down, and then see if we can work this out, okay?

I agree they are being a bit picky. And we have no guarantee that the next buyer won't be the same way. Let's get this thing done and over with, and simply offer them a credit toward the repairs at closing. That way you won't have to worry about making the repairs and coordinating all that. They can take care of it themselves.

I'm afraid all buyers are just as picky. And may I tell you what concerns me about not agreeing to do these repairs? The buyers could walk away free and clear from this contract, leaving you legally obligated to either fix these items, or disclose them to the next buyer. That'll put you in the same position you are now, only weeks or months later. Is that what you want?

It's possible. And, at the same time, when you go to buy your next house, won't you want these items to be in good condition as well?

I agree. And unfortunately, they're in a position to be picky. If they weren't the only offer we've had in months, we might be in a better position. So, you can either address these repairs, or let the buyer walk and hope another, less picky buyer comes along in the next three months Which do you prefer?

∽

5.   The buyer's just trying to get more money out of me.

Of course they are trying to get more money out of you. They have entered "the honeymoon's over" phase. You see, when they wrote the contract, they would have paid anything to have the house. Now that they see it's not perfect, they're backing off and getting what we call in the business "buyer's remorse." They're questioning their decision to the point that they want to be compensated for the repairs the house needs. We don't want them to walk, and I appreciate that you don't want to spend more money. Just imagine that we found a middle ground and everyone was happy. Wouldn't that be great?

It's not unusual that you would feel that way. After all, it's like we're going through a second negotiation all over again for the inspection issues, isn't it? And if I could make it go away, I would. Let's look at the facts. We have a house with some old wiring that could be unsafe. It's a liability to you if you stay here, and it's a liability to you if you sell it this way. If there's ever a problem in the future, it could come back to haunt you. Fixing the wiring is just protecting your own best interest. It truly benefits you to go ahead and do it, regardless of whether they take the house. Don't you agree?

It does seem that way, doesn't it? And yet, as it states in the standard provisions of the contract, as a seller you're obligated to transfer the house to them in safe operating condition. Would you consider these items to be safe and operating?

I can appreciate that you would feel that way. And, the buyers aren't actually asking you for any money. They're simply asking you to repair the items that are not safe and operating. They have kids, and just want to make sure its okay for them to live there. Let's do the right thing and make the repairs, okay?

I can see how you might think that. And really, it was me and their agent that thought a credit would be the easiest way to handle this. The buyer's would actually prefer the items be repaired prior to closing. So, clearly they're not looking for any money from you, okay?

I agree it sounds like they might be trying for more money. And, at the same time, that's a big gamble for them to take, isn't it? I mean, isn't it a little far fetched that they negotiate a price that you'll accept, and then hope there're enough items to repair on the home inspection where they could get a bunch of money back from you? Or, isn't it simply a case of these items showing up on the report and needing to be repaired?

∽

6.   If I do all this work, I might as well put it back on the market at a higher price.

Well, you could put it back on the market at a higher price. The only problem is that interest rates have gone up, and the market is headed down. Would you want to risk getting less for the house, or simply negotiate something that works for everyone?

So, if you put the house back on the market and it takes months to find another buyer, what is the impact of making double payments while the market drops? Right now, you have a buyer who will get you into the new house on time. Think about all the factors. Do you want to maintain two houses in the winter? Let's go ahead and negotiate the inspection, okay?

What we see, time and time again, is that a buyer will try to ask for everything under the sun, hoping that they will get it, and then get realistic when they find out that can't. So, just to show good faith, can you split it with them?

Sure, we can do that. But didn't you say you wanted to be in your new home soon? What if we put it back on the market at a higher price, and it sits there for another few months? There is still no guarantee of what price you will get. Meanwhile, by that time, you'll have spent the same amount in mortgage payments, utilities, taxes and insurance as you would have in just making the repairs and getting this deal closed. Shouldn't you just make these repairs?

I can understand your saying that. And, what it sounds like is you're just frustrated with the entire situation, and the buyers, aren't you? Look, I want to have you do what is in your best interest. So just imagine for a moment that you put it back on the market, and the next buyer is even worse than this one. What then? Do you really want to take that chance, or do you simply want to get the deal closed and move forward?

That makes sense. And since you're not adding a bedroom, bathroom, deck, hot tub or anything else that would be an addition, as opposed to just repairs, how will you justify the increase in price?

I see where you're going, and unfortunately it doesn't work that way. You lived in a house for 15 years. In that time, you had a functioning hot water heater. It is now not functioning properly, and contractually needs to be replaced. If you tried to sell a 15 year old car, would you be able to increase the price because the buyer wanted you to replace the 15 year old bald, worn out tires?

∽

7.   We already came off the price in negotiations, we're not giving anymore.

No problem. I don't want you to give more; I simply want you to be moved into your new house. The buyers negotiated you down in price to what you felt was your bottom line, and now they want even more. That doesn't seem fair, does it? And yet, we know that the first offer is usually the best offer. If we lose this buyer, the next offer may be lower. Is that a chance you want to take?

You're so right. It seems like they forgot you already came down in price, didn't they? So let's do this: I will refresh their memory, and let the agent know there's not much room to renegotiate. If they want the house, they will need to take on some of the work themselves, do you agree? And if they are willing to do some of the work, are you willing to do the rest?

I understand. And the buyers negotiated with you in good faith, based on the house not needing repairs. They had no way of knowing about the repairs needed, unless you would have told them up front. Do you want them to walk away over these repairs, or do you want the home sold?

I know you did. And I'll state your position to the buyer's agent. And when the buyer walks away from the sale, do you want to go back on the market with a lower price to reflect the repair items? Or, do you want me to call contractors so that you can get them repaired just in case we ever get another offer?

I don't want you to give anymore either. And I know you feel like you're already losing money. Unfortunately, these repairs are all very legitimate. If we say no, and the buyer cancels the contract, we will still have to either make the repairs, or disclose them to the next buyer. Since the first offer is generally the best offer, and the longer a home sits on the market the harder it becomes to sell, will you really be ahead by saying no?

I want you to trust me and make the repairs, because losing the sale and having to go back on the market raises a lot of red flags to buyers and other agents. And, it's likely that we'll be in the same position again, probably with an even lower contract price than this one, months from now. You don't want that, do you?

∽

"**N**oW What Do I Say?"

NEGOTIATING HOME INSPECTIONS - BUYERS

1.   These repairs are going to cost thousands.

Yes the repairs could cost thousands, and they may not. All we need to do at this point is get a licensed contractor to go take a look, and give us a written estimate. Then we can make an educated decision on how to proceed from there, okay?

I agree. The repairs could costs thousands. And has there ever been a time when something seemed like a much bigger deal when you first found out about it, because of emotional overload? Well, this time could be just like that time, may I explain? Once we break it down, it may not be as bad as the initial report seems. I bet between all of us, we can work something out that will be right for both you and the seller. Let's set up a time to have a conference call where we can all talk this through together, okay?

You may be right. I can only tell you from past history that these things almost always get worked out. It may seem overwhelming right now, but in the long run you'll find that they don't cost what you think they will, okay?

Wow, I certainly understand your concern! Instead of you spending thousands to have these items fixed, let's draw up an addendum and ask the seller to take responsibility for their own house. Does that make sense?

Yes they are and you know why that's the best thing for you? Think about this, the house you're buying is eighteen years old. There are bound to be some things in need of repair.

If you were buying this house a year ago, these items might have just barely passed inspection, and you'd be footing the bill now. Now, you get to relax knowing that you're going to have the items repaired or replaced by professionals, and it's not going to cost you anything. Isn't that great?

It's very possible. And the seller will need to repair or replace the important items, as per the contract. So, clearly it's better to find out now, rather than finding out after you close, right?

❧

2.   I don't want a credit. I want the seller to do all repairs.

You want the seller to make the repairs instead of your receiving the money at closing? I understand, and let me run something by you before we go back to them with that, okay? Imagine for a moment that you get the credit at closing. You have cash in hand to choose whatever contractor you want, you get to oversee the repairs personally and possibly save yourself money. Wouldn't that be a better situation than having the seller do it their way?

I want you to accept the credit. That way, you can choose your own contractor and watch over the repairs yourself, instead of us trusting that the seller will have it done to your satisfaction, okay?

Okay, but here is what sometimes happens. The seller might do the repairs as cheaply as possible so they can save some money. Is that what you really what? You can negotiate a fair credit, or risk having some sub-standard materials used by the seller to patch things up. Which do you prefer?

I totally understand. And has there ever been a time when you saw some work that looked a little shoddy? Well that could happen again, in this case, if the seller does it themselves, right? If you want the work done the way <u>you</u> want it, then you'll want to select the best professionals to do it, make sense?

Really? If you had three estimates for something that you're never going to see again, wouldn't you just take the cheapest one and not care about quality? That's who you want fixing the stuff in <u>your</u> new home? Let's just take the credit, which is for the average of the three estimates, and get someone in that you trust to do the work, all right?

You can do that, and you risk holding up the settlement. What if the repairs aren't finished by the time you get to closing? I mean, after you close, what incentive would the seller or the repair man have to finish the work? In that situation, the only thing you can do is delay closing. Do you want to risk that?

3.   **We want everything fixed on the home inspection list, or we're going to walk.**

I don't blame you. We weren't expecting any of this. So, now you know the house is not perfect. We can start over looking again and see if we can find a perfect house that needs nothing. Although, everything we've looked at needs work, doesn't it? In fact, a lot of the houses we've looked at need way more work than this one. Did you want to go back to one of those? I didn't think so. Look, as frustrating as this is, it's clearly the best that we've seen in the price range, and it would be a shame to lose it.

I understand you want everything fixed but it's like renegotiating the contract all over again! And, remember what we talked about when you first made an offer on this house? Decide what you want, and then make them an offer that you think will be a little too low but they might take it. It's just like making the initial offer. There should be some flexibility on both sides. Don't you agree?

Ok, we can try that. So, which one of the houses that you didn't like enough the first time around would you like to make an offer on?

That's a valid demand. However, I'm afraid you're going to be left disappointed, can I tell you why? Unless you buy new construction, every home out there will have things that need attention, or repair. Buyers typically understand this, and you're legally protected against major defaults. Do you really want to lose a $300,000 house over a cracked window pane and broken porch light?

I hear what you're saying, and we'll present that to the seller. They'll have the option to either agree to fix everything, or offer to only do what they're contractually obligated to do, which does give you the option to walk away. Let's see what they agree to do before we make any decisions on not buying the house, okay?

I understand your not wanting to take care of any of the repairs yourself. Let's take a moment to really go over the items and the numbers here. It does seem a bit overwhelming when you first look at the report. When we actually break it down, item by item, looking at the actual cost to repair, it isn't as bad as it first seems. Just remember we got a great deal on the home. You're going into it with instant equity already. You don't really want to lose this house over a few repairs, do you?

∽

4.   We don't believe the seller's estimates.

Well, the estimates are from reputable companies, so what specifically causes you to believe they're not valid? These companies have been in business for a long time and would not undervalue their services. As a matter of fact, most times they will estimate high. So, if you were to see this house for the first time, and knew you would get a credit of $5,000, you'd probably jump on it, right? Don't you think other buyers will feel the same?

I know. It's really easy to get caught up in who has the right numbers to correct the problem. The seller has his estimates, and you have your estimates. So, let's do this: let's take all the estimates and do an average. That way it's fair for everybody, make sense?

Okay. And you know they didn't just make them up, right? Why don't I give you copies so you can see for yourself? And if you're still not happy, then you or I can call the repairmen personally and find out the information we need. Will that work?

I understand. So then, let's get our own. I have a list of professional contractors for you to choose from, or did you have someone in mind? Either way, to keep everyone honest, we're going to need at least two of our own estimates. Do you want me to just go down my list, or would you like to make the calls?

Okay. And I want to make sure you're confident with what you're doing here. So let's get the licensed contractor to give us a written estimate, showing that he will actually do the repairs for the amount they are offering, okay?

I understand how you feel. And since this is all that the seller is willing to do, we can either accept their offer, or we can have our own licensed contractor give an estimate and go from there. Which is better for you?

❧

5.   Why didn't the seller disclose this?

Well, I don't know the answer to that. They may have not been paying attention to the questions. I see these forms all the time where the sellers leave a line blank, or forget to check something. Let's send the form back over and ask them to fill it out again with a very detailed description of what happened. That way you can feel comfortable that this will be handled correctly. Will that be all right?

Truly, we don't know if they just forgot about it, or took it for granted. Here is what I want you to remember: you're not moving in with them, and you will never see them again after you buy the home. Let's separate our feelings about how lame they are, from our feelings about this incredible home. Your relationship with them will be over in sixty days, but this could be your house forever, right?

I really don't know. They may not have known about it until the inspection came up. Tell you what, let me ask the listing agent what happened and go from there. Most likely it wasn't known, and we can certainly have the inspector go back again if you have any doubts. Will that work for you?

I have no idea, and I can call their agent and ask. Although, I highly doubt that they'd be up front about why they were hiding something, if, in fact, they actually were hiding something, don't you think? Either way, it's on the report and they have to have it professionally repaired or give you the money to get it done yourself, okay?

That's a great question, and I don't know the answer to it. They either didn't know about it themselves, or they thought they could get one over on us. Either way we have two options. We can either walk away from the house, or we can ask them to fix it, or credit you the money to fix it, after closing. Which is better for you?

Maybe they just totally forgot about it all together. Let's give them the benefit of the doubt, and just ask them to fix it, or credit us the money to have it fixed. In the end, that's all you really want, isn't it?

☙

Donna Fleetwood is a veteran real estate agent who has consistently sold over 100 homes a year. Donna spent several years in an intense training program to hone her objection handling skills and has written hundreds of objection handlers. Partnering with Scott and Christy was the natural outcome of that study. Donna credits the growth of her business to knowing what to say and how to say it.

Christy Crouch has been in real estate for over eighteen years and has studied objection handlers from her first year in the business. Christy consistently sells over 100 homes per year and utilizes these objection handlers in her business day after day. After studying practicing and teaching objection handlers for so many years, Christy is excited to bring you this book knowing that using it will help you take your business to new heights.

Scott Friedman was a top producing real estate agent for over eight years. Now he is a professional speaker, a certified professional coach and a master of objection handlers. Co-owner of You're The Difference Sales Training and Coaching, Scott has been coaching real estate agents and teaching objection handlers for over six years. Scott is committed to helping you take your business to the next level, and knows *Now What Do I Say?* is the first step towards your success.